⬢ TDK
SPECIAL OCCASION
VIDEO GUIDE

✧ TDK
SPECIAL OCCASION
VIDEO GUIDE

by

Basil Lane

COPYRIGHT © BASIL LANE 1987
ALL RIGHTS RESERVED

First published in Great Britain by
Phoenix Publishing Associates Ltd

ISBN 0 9465 7675 0

Published by Phoenix Publishing Associates
14, Vernon Rd, Bushey, Herts WD2 2JL

Edited by Red Herring Publishing Ltd
83/84 Long Acre, London WC2E 9NG

Book design by Troika Graphics

Photography by David Redfern, Steve Hawkins, Peter Herring
and Suzie Gibbons

Cover Photograph by David Redfern

Typeset by Basil Lane

Printed in Great Britain by Adlards & Son Ltd., The Garden City Press, Letchworth, Herts.

ACKNOWLEDGEMENTS

To Mr and Mrs Reece for permission to record and photograph their wedding. To TDK (UK) Ltd and THORN EMI Ferguson for their technical assistance.

CONTENTS

	Introduction	7
Chapter 1	The Joys and Hazards of Making a Video	9
Chapter 2	About Video Equipment	19
Chapter 3	Cameras, Lighting and Sound	39
Chapter 4	Planning for a Wedding Shoot	57
Chapter 5	The Elements of Camera Technique	73
Chapter 6	The Great Day!	83
Chapter 7	Post-production Preparations	97
Chapter 8	Adding the Professional Touch	111
Chapter 9	The Oops! Factor	129
Chapter 10	High-days and Holidays	147
	Glossary	156
	Technical Appendix	167
	Index	174

Introduction

Suddenly, everyone wants to make a video recording of their wedding! It is not entirely coincidence that one of the most successful of recent video films was of the wedding of Prince Andrew and Sarah Ferguson. The public interest in this, the wedding of 1986, was so great that it influenced the wedding dress design of many a young girl, but at the same time evoked an enormous interest in the use of video cameras as a way of making a valued and permanent record of a happy event.

This book is a simple guide which will help the novice to use video cameras and other video equipment to make a professional-looking record of a family event. The wedding has been chosen as the principal practical example since it offers the greatest challenge to the budding cameraperson.

However, this book is definitely not a catalogue of the technical 'works' of a camera, recorder, or anything else. Instead it is a simple description of how to put a 'film' together, using the kind of equipment typically available for hire or purchase from a local TV and video rental shop. Some parts of the book are intended for the more advanced enthusiast and deal with the more exotic kinds of cameras and editing equipment. Nevertheless, these are not essential to the main theme, which is to show how it is possible to make a polished production, using the modern video equivalent of a 'Box Brownie'!

It is never possible to obtain good results from any camera without gaining experience through experiment. This is why the reader should resolve to practice making a video film before attempting to record an event like a wedding, where the action can never be repeated.

Do not let this deter you - with good planning and preparation, plus a little imagination, there is no reason why your record should not be just as satisfying.

Above all, it does not cost much - and the end product is easily duplicated for distribution among friends and relatives.

Have fun!

1
The Joys and Hazards of Making a Video

Special Occasion Video Guide

WEDDING FILM NOTES

Bride's name: Yvonne Middleton
Address: 22, Field View Rd, SW18. Tel: 01-887 1111
Notes: House with good window light, situated 2 miles from church. Will travel by Rolls to the church with father.

Groom's name: Brian Smith
Address: Flat H, 19 South Rd, SW18. Tel: 01-887 9999
Notes: Flat no good for filming - poor light and too messy! Groom putting up best man and departing for church by taxi.

Bride's mum would like film taken before wedding, during preparations. Arrive 2hrs before time of wedding. Must film bride's sister coming from Canada for the event.

Church: St.Albans, Christian Rd SW18.
Vicar: Rev. Williams, lives in vicarage next to church. OK to film in church - don't film in vestry during signing of register. Don't go inside altar rails. CHURCH HAS STAINED GLASS at altar end - white glass everywhere else. Good light during visit. OK to place mic stand in choir stalls. Car Parking difficult.

Reception Rooms: The Clarion Pub (1 mile on Christian Rd from church). Parking good. Room a large church hall-type place - avoid loo notice on one side when filming in room.

Lighting good but watch if poor light and fluorescent lights switched on - test!

Sit-down meal planned, all speeches from top table into microphone on stand behind table. Can attach video mic to stand and string cable without problems of guests tripping - providing film from stage left side of hall.

Wedding timed to take place at 3.15pm, reception at 4.15pm. Reception finishes at 8.00pm. No need to wait to the end!

Contact wedding photographer to get cooperation and tips on good points for camera. (Local knowledge of church and hall).

The notes produced as part of our wedding shoot planning.

The Joys and Hazards of Making a Video

To make a good video film two basic problems must be solved, the first and most obvious of which is to become acquainted with some of the technicalities and all of the possibilities of the equipment.

All too often, the novice film maker can suffer disappointments, simply because a camera battery has not been recharged, or unfamiliarity with the legends on the camera buttons leads to the wrong thing being pressed!

Equally important, and often overlooked, is the need to carefully plan the film. Good planning can make sure that every important event is covered without technical hitches. That way, simple details such as getting from A to B fast enough to film the complete wedding can be anticipated and allowed for.

This book is intended to help you through every aspect of making a video film and there are some useful short-cuts which may help you get familiar with the subject (and the jargon) more quickly.

I have tried to divide the book into two parallel parts. One is concerned with technique - the sort used by all good film makers around the world; the other deals with the technology of video recording and its associated equipment.

The chapter headings will give you a good guide on the particular subject covered and wherever possible I have tried to employ everyday terms and avoid bewildering 'techno-speak'. However, some jargon inevitably has to be used and this does pose problems.

First, making video recordings using a camera is a relatively new process, but many of the terms and expressions have been 'borrowed' from the older photographic film making industry.

This produces some oddities - such as the way we are forced to refer to a video film - as opposed to the sort of video recording we make at home from TV programmes.

The second problem is the new terminology originating from the world of video technology.

To provide a rapid route to understanding the more technical terms I have been forced to use, a comprehensive glossary is provided at the

Special Occasion Video Guide

back of the book.

Also, for ease of reference, the first time any such term appears it will be printed in italics.

But let us return to the subject of the preparations needed to produce a wedding video. Although I have indicated some elementary considerations, there is actually more to it than traffic, road conditions and the type of transport available.

There will also be the matter of fighting through guests to get into the church after recording the arrival of the bride and her father, in order to film their walk up the aisle.

Or what about the more simple difficulties of parking your car easily and quickly when moving from one location to the next?

All the way through this book, you will see that a dedicated and determined approach to the task will avoid all but the most unpredictable of problems.

Your initial efforts should include attendance at rehearsals and any planning meetings organised by the parents as part of the preparations for the ceremony and the reception.

The sort of difficulty you might meet on the day itself could range from a human and very funny incident, through to some kind of technical disaster. It is to be hoped that the latter is not something that happens to you!

One difficulty I encountered which might serve as an example of the unexpected was an occasion when I was recording a wedding taking place at a church with a particularly capacious porch.

As it was raining, many of the arriving guests were sheltering in the porch, waiting for their first glimpse of the bride. Also present was myself, posing as an intrepid and 'professional' cameraman, and the vicar.

What few of us had realised was that the porch was also the home for a flock of pigeons which, at the worst possible moment, started fluttering over the vicar's head.

Fortunately, the shot being filmed at that moment (intended to be of an expectant and reverent vicar) was turned into something even more welcome. In his attempts to get rid of the pestilential pigeons, he thrashed around quite wildly, producing considerable amusement and laughter from the waiting guests!

Through no planning of my own, a totally unplanned scene was added to the recording, to be much appreciated by the bride and groom when they saw the finished tape some weeks later.

However, the real point to be returned to yet again is that good planning takes time and care. It can even help you to acquire assurance and self-confidence about your final decisions when the unexpected happens in the more hectic moments of the wedding.

So why not start planning right now - perhaps even before you have selected the video equipment to be used.

Preliminary notes

An excellent starting point is to set down some rough notes about the couple, the family and the guests. The correct spelling of names is important, since they might be needed in the titles. Also, get a blank sample of the wedding invitation, as it might serve as almost complete artwork for the opening sequence of the video film.

In the case of the wedding used for the photographs in this book, the very first sketchy notes were in the form of a questionnaire.

It is an example of the sort of thing which can be used at any other wedding or, with some modifications, at other family events to be filmed. As a matter of course, it should also carry details about the locations.

Thus, the location of the church, reception rooms and the home addresses of the bride and groom are included, as are notes about parking difficulties or architectural features of the church which can be used for atmosphere shots on or before the day itself.

With this information noted down, it becomes quite easy to check travelling times from one location to another as well as designing the basis of the *storyboard* of the video recordings to be made on the wedding day.

By the way, in noting down

Special Occasion Video Guide

travelling times, don't forget that the traffic conditions will change from day to day, and even with the time of day!

Tell the 'actors' the plans!

Generally the bride, the groom and their families, will know of your plan to film the wedding, so it makes sense to discuss their own particular preferences. This will help to ensure that you record key events that will make the film special to them. Indeed, as soon as possible, consult them about your timetable for the whole event.

Let us take an example of the sort of thing that is useful.

The table on page 10, is a rough guide which might have been compiled in your first meetings. It must be checked and corrected using the experience gained from trial journeys, and from learning about the pace of the ceremony as observed in any rehearsals.

One thing that also starts to emerge from compiling a table like this is the impossibility for a single cameraperson to cover all of the key moments listed. Some choice has to be made, and this can be done in conjunction with the bride and groom.

In reality then, this initial timetable is no more than a list of suggestions which will have to be refined as more knowledge is gained of the filming locations.

A typical example of the sort of thing that will emerge from a scouting trip to the church is the existence of balconies that might offer a good viewpoint - providing that access is simple and there is no disturbance to the service.

This is where it is absolutely vital to secure the cooperation of the vicar. After all, he may have a distinct aversion to the extra lighting sometimes needed in a dark church. He might even want to lay down a few rules for the video camera crew, to ensure they avoid disturbing the more sacred parts of the ceremony.

Rehearsals, or at the very least, a preview visit to the church will be useful to check the amount of light available for filming, find unusual camera locations and to seek suitable places for any extra microphones that may be needed.

At the same time, draw little thumbnail sketches of the church and grounds that show tested camera and microphone locations for use on the day.

Prepare for the unexpected

Before getting too far into the planning for the film, it will become obvious that an assistant will be not so much useful as essential.

Every video film maker should seriously consider working with a reliable friend. He, or she, can at least take charge of carrying the bag of accessories and spare tapes, and also might be given the vital job of making a separate so-called 'wild' sound recording.

Just to quickly clarify this bit of jargon, a *wild sound recording* is one made by a tape or cassette recorder that is in no way connected to the camera.

It is probably one of the most valuable aids to polishing the final production, since the recording can often be used to act as a bridge between successive scenes that might

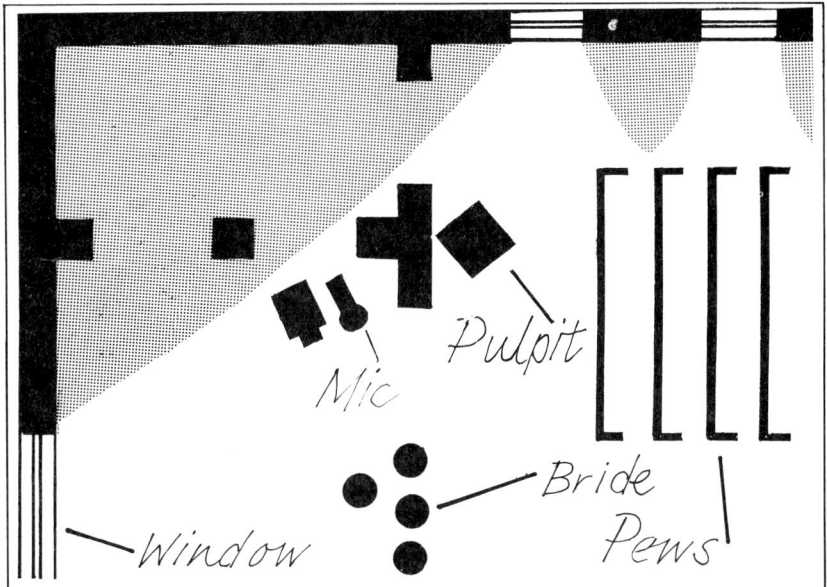

Typical plan view diagrams that may be noted down prior to filming.

Special Occasion Video Guide

A short storyboard for the sequences where the participants' positions can be predicted.

otherwise appear disjointed.

Take for example, the problems facing the cameraperson who first films the arrival of the bride and her father at the church, and then has to dash to an inside vantage point to film the walk up the aisle. In the time taken by this dash, the bride may be halfway to the altar!

This jump can be masked if a wild sound recording of the church organ is being made continuously and later *dubbed* on to the final version of the video.

Similarly, the same technique can be used outside the church when the newly-weds emerge and the cameraperson is busily trying to get a series of short shots from different angles.

A continuous sound-track from a separate wild recording helps to give the badly needed *continuity,* and covers up the gaps between one scene and the next.

The storyboard

For those readers used to taking just a 35mm camera to a wedding to take snaps of the happy event, all this careful and detailed planning may seem unnecessary.

However, the truth is that a video recording is always studied more critically than a simple photograph. Attention to detail at an early stage will always show in the finished product.

The storyboard technique is an indispensable part of this process. It is certainly an important part of any professional production, although it is more often used at times where events can be controlled. It is also a useful way for the film director - when there is one - and the cameraperson to exchange ideas.

So what exactly is a storyboard? In simple terms it is a sort of strip cartoon of the key scenes to be taken in the film. It can also can be a series of instructional sketches or plans which show the locations of the camera and the scene to be recorded.

The important thing to realise is that the storyboard is more significant in scripted and pre-planned productions, and therefore might be most practical for the in-church scenes.

Plan diagrams, on the other hand, are merely technical 'notes' reminding the film maker of the best locations and lighting conditions that might help or interfere with the shoot.

The purpose of the storyboard is that it should clearly show the camera angles needed, and how much of the background is to be included.

This is a particularly useful note, as most video cameras have lenses which can zoom in and out of a scene to frame detail, or take in a broad view of the action.

Remember, on the day itself you may only get one opportunity to capture many of the key shots, so planning for these is essential.

Of course, spontaneous events do happen at a wedding that need to be filmed but which obviously cannot be included in the storyboard.

Nevertheless, it can still play a useful role in guiding both the camera operator and assistant, in the heat of the moment. It also serves as a handy memorandum for use during the final post production stages of the video recording.

EQUIPMENT USED FOR MR. & MRS REECE'S WEDDING

C-format VHS camcorder
Standard VHS camcorder
Cardiod directional microphone
Hypercardiod directional microphone
Extension microphone cable
Spare battery packs (fully charged)
Two E180 cassettes (TDK EHG)
Microphone stand
Tripod
Notebook and pen
Lightweight stepladder (emergencies only!)
Plastic insulating tape
String.

2
About Video Equipment

Special Occasion Video Guide

Video photography is a new technology that is fast becoming a popular source of entertainment for many people. The equipment is now easier to use, and offers many of the features that have been available on still cameras for some time.

Like the still camera, video cameras are available in a variety of models ranging from the automated 'point and shoot' type, through to more complex versions which will appeal to the more ambitious enthusiast.

Information which helps in the process of familiarisation with video will prove useful. It can be bypassed, but on the other hand may well provide valuable clues to irritating effects that could emerge on tape in special, but quite regularly encountered circumstances.

For most users, the first experience of video photography will probably be with equipment hired from the local TV rental shop.

These days, most offer cameras and portable recorders, or combination machines called *camcorders*. Almost all of these use the same type of tape cassette as the home video recorder.

There are two exceptions to this rule. The first is a variant

VHS, Beta and C-format cassettes compared.

of the VHS tape format called VHS C, or Compact. The tapes made by this type of machine can be replayed on existing standard VHS machines by using a simple and inexpensive mechanical adaptor, described in more detail elsewhere in this book.

The second type belongs to the *8mm video* system, a name coined to describe the width of the magnetic tape used in its video cassettes. Although some versions have been made offering the features of a full domestic VCR, these are comparatively rare.

8mm and Beta Video

The basic standards for this new format have been agreed by a large number of companies. Sony and Akai were among the first to introduce machines but are being rapidly followed by many other companies.

The difference between 8mm video and the earlier *Beta* and *VHS* formats is that the tape cassette is incompatible with both. A video recorded on an 8mm camera has to be replayed on an 8mm machine.

Of course, it is equally true that a Beta or VHS tape has to be played back on machines of a similar standard, but because there are many more of these in use, there is a better chance that the video photographer will be able to replay the tape without having to tote his own equipment around relatives!

This is not to denigrate the 8mm system, which offers some interesting new features, but merely to point out that for the novice it can be an inconvenient format to choose.

The 8mm system also suffers from one other disadvantage, which makes it unsuitable for use when the final result is to be edited and polished to simulate professional results.

The system is designed in such a way that when the sound and picture image are recorded on the cassette, they are inextricably linked. This makes the possibility of editing the sound using *audio dubbing* techniques - or even adding some sound later - extremely difficult.

Just why this sort of manipulation may be a necessary part of video film making, will be explained in more detail later.

Special Occasion Video Guide

The practical examples of video photography in this book are based entirely on the VHS tape format, and there are very good reasons for this.

The VHS tape format

Over eighty per cent of British households using video have adopted the VHS system for their home video equipment. Cameras based on the VHS system are readily hired from local TV rental shops and finally, a great range of camera systems can be easily bought which will match the needs of either the amateur first-time film maker, or the more advanced and ambitious enthusiast.

The Beta video format invented by Sony, offers high quality recordings, but is now generally in decline, and fewer cameras are available. Those that are available may not offer features regularly found in the VHS system.

However, the general operation of all video systems is similar, and the process of making an 8mm or Beta video film uses the same film-making techniques as VHS - or for that matter the methods employed by a real filmmaker!

A final word on tape compatibility. As mentioned earlier, the inventors of the VHS system have introduced a second type of cassette, called the Compact, or *C-format.*

The dimensions of the tape itself are the same as for a full sized cassette; it is merely that the cassette housing has been made smaller to fit into a new generation of very light and portable camcorders.

A C-format VHS cassette can be replayed in any ordinary VHS player, simply by popping it into a special adaptor which converts it to the dimensions of the full size cassette. These adaptors are readily available, not too expensive and very easy to use.

The only limitation of the C-format VHS tape is that the maximum recording time available is thirty minutes at Standard speeds, one hour in Long Play mode. This is not a problem for the video photographer as the number of times a thirty minute tape will be inadequate for an event are very rare indeed.

More than a home movie

Because it is in the nature of a

About Video Equipment

video recording that it can be instantly replayed in colour and with sound as well, the entire process is much easier than making a home movie. At its most basic, all that is needed is a video camera and recorder!

Nevertheless, the professional touches that become desirable as you gain experience, can now be added to a home video using one or more of the wide range of accessories available for video photographers.

These range from simple devices such as a highly directional microphone, or at the other extreme, a complex editing desk for post-production work.

Used sensibly, any of these extra components can help to create a polished final product which carries many of the hallmarks of the professional video unit.

Although the video cameras and recorders that can be hired from TV rental shops are generally the simpler 'point and shoot' variety, the advice and information here will be of help both to the first time user and the more ambitious.

For this reason, features available at both ends of the spectrum are described.

But, before getting into this kind of detail, let us start with a very simple outline of the

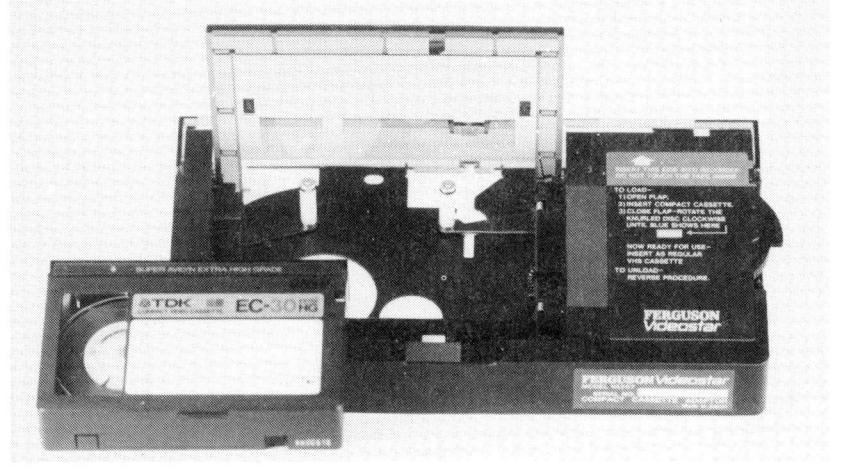

The smaller C-format cassette fits inside the adaptor to form a complete standard cassette.

23

Special Occasion Video Guide

way a video camera works. This will help to provide some confidence when encountering the 'jargon' language of video photography.

The video camera lens

The best starting point is the lens. This is usually of a variable focal length type, and will *zoom* from *wide angle* to *telephoto*, either manually or powered from the camera at the touch of a button.

Another feature of most zoom lenses is the ability to be operated in a *macro* mode.

This is where the focal length is adjusted to view very small and close objects, often magnifying them greatly - a real boon for the nature enthusiast!

It could also be used to obtain a close-up of the wedding ring, in a contrived moment during the wedding reception.

Although a few cameras have special lenses which need no focusing, the majority have this function. Here too, a manual or power-driven option is offered. However, auto-focusing has both drawbacks as well as advantages to be taken into consideration.

The nature of these limitations will depend on the way in which the camera automates the focusing process.

Some cameras work on the principle of looking for a vertical or horizontal line somewhere in the centre of the image. It will then try to make this as sharp as possible.

But suppose, for artistic reasons, the photographer wants to offset the image to one side - the focusing mechanism is perhaps now concentrating on a background element of the picture, and will re-focus to this, putting the wanted objects out of focus!

A typically annoying example of this type of system error is where the photographer may be shooting a scene through an open window framed by a window box - but really wants to film objects some yards away in the garden.

If the camera is moved to include too much of the window

About Video Equipment

frame or the flowers in the window box, the focus may unexpectedly jump to sharpen up the nearer objects, spoiling the focus of the subject proper.

This same kind of focusing mechanism can become wholly confused if the surface in view has no well defined lines. In this case, the focusing device will vainly hunt to and fro, trying to make sense of the image!

Additionally, the sort of focusing system just described will only work in good light.

If you are likely to want to film regularly in marginal light conditions, alternative focusing mechanisms may prove preferable. These use ultrasonic sound or infra-red light as a sort of radar system.

However, they too have limitations in that again, they may be affected by the wanted image being offset in the field of view.

Whatever the problems with auto-focusing, they can be easily overcome by switching to manual control on those occasions when the system needs to be overridden.

Even with just the ability to change focus or zoom from telephoto to wide angle, it is possible to exercise quite a lot of professional and artistic control over the recorded scenes.

Nevertheless, it may be an advantage to use some other tricks with lenses that may be seen in professional productions.

Fortunately, camera manufacturers also offer lens accessories which may be useful for special occasions.

A zoom lens in wide-angle view may produce this scene.

After zooming to telephoto, the same scene looks like this. The camera has not been moved.

25

These range from additions which extend the wide angle, telephoto or macro features, to special filters which give *starburst*, *soft-focus* or other visual effects.

In all cases, these devices must be used judiciously, and after some experiment. If used carelessly or too often, they can mar the recording which, after all, is not a romantic epic but first and foremost an accurate documentary of a special occasion.

Sensing the image

The lens of a video camera focuses the image on to a device which will convert the light, shade and colour into an electronic signal which can be recorded on to tape.

Until recent years, this has been done by a component made in the form of a glass tube, coated at one end with light sensitive material. This, with the rest of the tube components, turns the image into a video signal.

There are two varieties of this component called respectively, *Newvicon* and *Saticon* tubes and the literature accompanying the camera will give some idea of their low light sensitivity, using a measurement system scaled in units called *lux*.

This is no place to go into a deep discussion of the measurement of light levels, but suffice it to say that the smaller the lux number for the camera, the more successful it is at recording in low light conditions!

As a useful guide to the lux range of different types of lighting, the chart above, illustrates the normal range of values that might be encountered.

More recently, something called a *CCD* - (it means charge coupled device) - has been emerging as a popular alternative to the tube.

In essence this is a specially designed semiconductor chip which can operate like a tube, and may be more sensitive in low light conditions. The resolution of fine detail is sometimes a problem for CCD devices, so where this is important to the user, it is best to compare the two types of camera in use on an object containing fine detail.

A simple guide to the quality

About Video Equipment

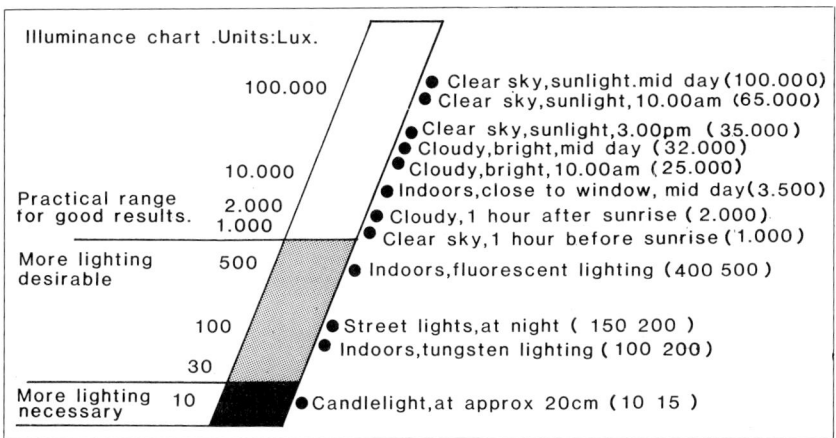

of a camera's performance in this respect is the number of horizontal TV lines the system can resolve.

Typically, a broadcast camera resolves at least the 625 lines seen on the television screen, and usually can do much better than this.

Domestic cameras vary in their resolution down to as low as 200 lines. Essentially, the more lines resolved, the more detailed the image will appear.

The amount of light falling on the image sensor is always important. It is not just a question of the minimum light levels that can be sensed, but also the maximum. Like a still film camera, the range of *contrast* and *brightness* of the image falling on the sensor has to be exactly right.

Video cameras are fitted with a light level sensor to do this job. This is coupled to an electrically-driven *iris* in the lens which opens up in low light conditions, to provide exactly the right image brightness on the sensor.

Similarly, it will close down to reduce the light levels on the tube or CCD image sensor when the scene is too bright.

However, like the case of the automated focusing system, there are limitations which must be remembered.

First, some image sensors can be damaged by receiving too much light. The iris system cannot

The range of lighting values a video photographer might encounter.

Special Occasion Video Guide

always cope with extreme conditions and so, as a general rule, the camera should never be pointed into the sun or at a similarly bright light, unless you are certain of the tolerance of the image sensor.

Second, even when the brightest light source in the scene is below the point of damaging the sensor, it might still produce odd comet-like tails. These show up as a faint streak of light on the screen that appears when the camera is *panned*. It starts at the original position of the light source on the screen and links to the latest position of the light.

The effect is transitory, but nevertheless may prove annoying. It only happens with certain types of tube sensor, so if it is observed during tests, try to avoid holding the camera on such a light source in a real filming situation.

The auto-iris suffers from problems comparable to those of the autofocus and light sensing systems. Typically, it can set itself incorrectly where there are big differences between the brightness of the wanted parts of the picture compared to foreground or background.

As an appropriate example, many churches have white walls which may form the background to distance shots where the bride and groom occupy only a small part of the picture.

In this case, the iris mechanism may preferentially adjust the camera sensitivity to cope with the white wall, leaving the central figures as dark silhouettes!

Most cameras offer a limited solution to this dilemma, but it is far from a complete answer.

It is true that all cameras offer some indication of over- or under-light conditions, but in this case, the light levels may be perfectly suitable for the image sensor - but simply too contrasty for good results. Here, the photographer has to get used to careful observation in the viewfinder.

When overall light levels are too low for satisfactory recording, the camera offers a message in the viewfinder indicating a difficulty, but fails to give an idea of what would happen if the user were to go ahead and continue recording.

In fact, the first signs of poor quality pictures at low light levels arise in the colour part of the picture - something not seen through a *monochrome* viewfinder!

An effect called *chroma noise* starts to appear. It is first seen in *saturated colours* such as reds and blues and makes the scene appear as if seen through a coloured rainstorm. As light levels get lower, colours get distorted and the picture may well become totally unacceptable.

However, there are some cases where chroma noise can be acceptable, and the photographer can continue filming with impunity.

A typical instance of where this knowledge might be of value is a firework party. Here, the fireworks are certainly bright enough to be recorded, but the surrounding scene is well below the capability of the camera to resolve.

It is really going to be a matter of experiment and experience on the part of the photographer which will affect the decision whether to go ahead with the filming or not. Since tape is cheap and can be re-used, it is usually worth experimenting. The results can often be surprisingly rewarding.

To check out the likelihood of any of these technical problems arising, take every opportunity to attend wedding rehearsals. Bear in mind though the weather may be different, giving changed lighting conditions.

Similarly, the bride, the groom, bridesmaids and the clergyman will be wearing different clothes which may alter the way the automated systems of the camera behave.

Colour temperature

Before leaving the subject of the image sensor, there is one other important consideration worth bearing in mind.

This is what most camera manuals call *colour temperature,* an ugly technical term which usually leaves most people totally baffled!

It refers to the colour of the light that illuminates the scene. For example, very few artificial lights produce light of the same colour as the sun.

Special Occasion Video Guide

From ordinary bulbs, the light is usually more yellow; from fluorescent tubes, it can be sometimes pink, blue or even produce a green cast.

Normally, the eye does not notice this and compensates for the effect - but a video camera works in a different kind of way.

The reason for the rather odd use of the expression 'colour temperature' is because most light comes from materials that have become so hot they are incandescent.

This has resulted in a scale of colour temperatures expressed in units of degrees Kelvin.

At the low end of the scale, the yellowest and weakest light that might be registered is that of a candle. Further up the scale are ordinary light bulbs, quartz halogen light, fluorescent lighting and finally, the bluest and hottest colour temperature, that of daylight.

Clearly, the colour of these lights will affect the colours of the scene being illuminated, and some sort of correction will be needed. Fortunately, video cameras can do this in most cases but there are exceptions - as with most automated systems.

The main exception is fluorescent light which may add a green cast to the picture - or worse still produce an electrical interference which could affect the recording!

Once again, the value of experiment cannot be over-emphasised since it could prevent irreparable dis-appointments.

There may be some occasions when the camera recognises the change in light colour but will then prompt the photographer to make an adjustment.

This can be done either by pressing a button to switch a filter, or by getting the camera to take action automatically by pointing the lens at a white surface illuminated by the light in question, and then pressing a *white balance* button.

A few manufacturers make life a little simpler by providing a white filter to clip over the lens during the balancing process.

The sound system

About Video Equipment

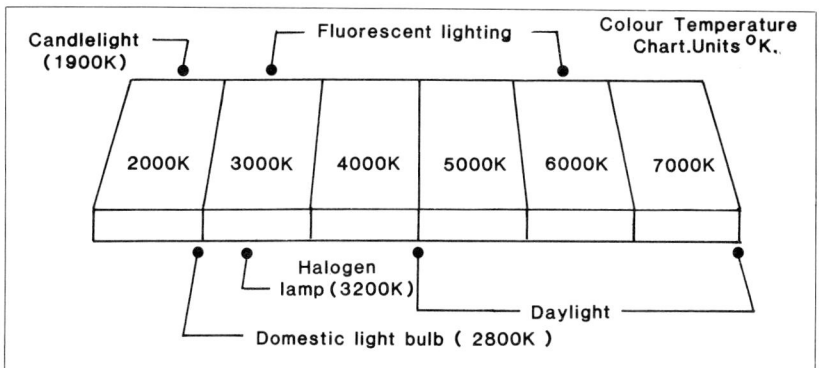

One of the beauties of video recording is that the sound can be recorded at the same time. It can also be edited or added to later, without affecting the picture image.

All video cameras, camcorders and recorders use automatic systems to ensure the right level is recorded on the tape. However, the sound at the tape may not be the one you want and it is worth examining why this is so.

Most cameras come with what is called an *omni-directional microphone*. This means it will pick up sounds all around, including odd noises made by the photographer! You could wind up with your own voice on the tape, giving instructions to your assistant.

True, this may not be a problem where you intend deliberately replacing the sound track with a recording made on another machine, but it should be borne in mind.

The all-round sensitivity of an omni-directional miucrophone is more of a nuisance where the wanted sound is in front of the camera, but is masked by much louder sounds coming from behind.
The automatic level adjustment system cannot differentiate between the wanted and the unwanted sound, and will make an annoyingly simple judgement to record everything at the maximum level for the tape.
The solution to the problem may well be to use a different microphone - perhaps even one held by an assistant. (It also explains why television reporters are often seen

The range of colour temperatures produced by various lighting conditions.

31

pointing a microphone at the person they are interviewing.)

Some microphones having directional properties are often available as a camera accessory. This is particularly useful where the photographer has no assistant, and therefore has to mount the microphone on the camera. A highly directional microphone is essential in such cases since it will preferentially pick up sound from the same direction as the camera viewpoint.

Something that becomes very obvious when listening to recorded sound is that a microphone does not behave in the same way as our sense of hearing.

It will detect and record every reverberation and echo from the room, or may even give the impression that sounds recorded in the open air are very dead.

In the case of our hearing, the brain compensates and discriminates between different sound sources around us so that we can extract the maximum information possible.

This is something which sound engineers call the 'cocktail party effect'. Somehow, we always manage to sort out the conversation we want from the babble of sound around us.

We achieve this partly by turning our head so that our ears are pointing in the right direction, and partly with some very clever and unnoticed activity in the brain.

Sound recording equipment cannot do this because it lacks such sophistication. Some allowances need to be made for this situation, either through exploiting the characteristics of directionally sensitive microphones, or by getting the microphone closer to the source.

Video equipment manufacturers also provide for this eventuality by offering microphones which can be connected to the camera system by a long lead.

This is a real boon on the occasions when the camera is confined to the back of a church but the user still wants to record something softly spoken, such as the responses from the bride and groom.

A discreetly - located separate mic on a stand near the couple, with a cable run to the back of

Take the opportunity to check the lighting in the church in advance, remembering that on the day you may not have sunlight around the altar, and additionally will have to contend with the presence of a congregation. Make sure, therefore, that you also attend the wedding rehearsal.

At some weddings, such as this Greek Orthodox service below, the congregation are encouraged to surround the bride and groom and to carry lit candles. This situation will give you a different set of problems to overcome (especially as your camera will be most sensitive to the bright flame if on auto setting). One solution is to seek out a high vantage point, such as a balcony, and film the whole scene, making the most of both candles and congregation. Above: If you have been lucky enough to station a second camera looking down the nave of the church, remember that lighting conditions facing this direction could be very different from the view towards the altar. It is unlikely you will be allowed much, if any, artificial lighting here since it would dazzle both couple and congregation.

the church can be quickly plugged in at the right moments.

This gives mobility to the camera when needed, since it will then be using its own microphone, and the right sound levels at critical moments from the second mic.

Fortunately, all this can be easily checked out on the spot because most cameras have a headphone socket. A few simple experiments will determine the best solution to each problem.

Some expensive cameras offer the possibility of recording the sound in *stereo*. The microphone looks very much the same as any other, but is actually two units in one.

Because the socket it plugs into is specially designed, it will only fit the right way round, with the two sections pointing right and left.

However if it, or another stereo microphone is used separately, it is important to make sure that the directions of sensitivity are pointed correctly, laterally left and right and not up and down!

The power supply

All camcorders and cameras need a power supply, normally provided via a battery pack. In the case of the camcorder it is attached to the machine, but where a camera is linked to a separate recorder power is provided by batteries in the recorder.

There are sometimes other possibilities of obtaining power

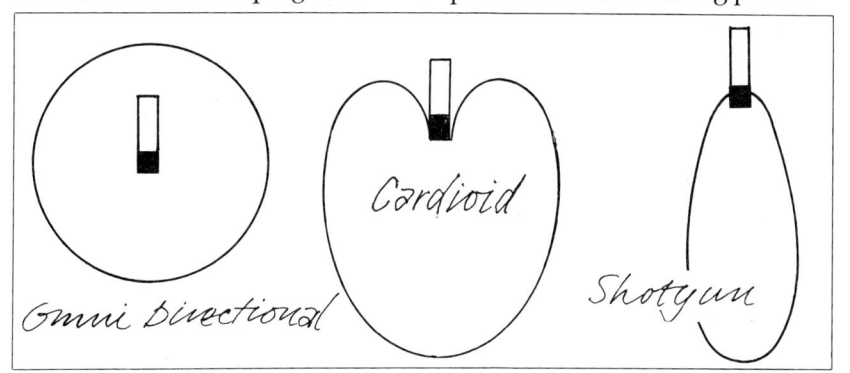

The field of relative sensitivity of an omni-directional microphone. This is called a polar diagram.

The polar diagram for a cardioid mic. This is slightly directional.

The very directional polar pattern of a hyper-cardiod or shotgun microphone.

Special Occasion Video Guide

from a mains adaptor unit, or even an adaptor plugged into the cigarette lighter of a car! However, both of these limit the photographer, through the need for a lead connecting the system to the power source.

Where batteries are provided, they should be fully charged, and checked to find out how long they will last for both recording, and for running the preview circuits in the camera system.

Spares, or larger capacity batteries are an important accessory that should not be overlooked.

A two-hour battery may seem long enough to record a two-hour event but in practice, because of the circuits in the camera that may be operative even when not recording, it could require up to three or four hours capacity to cope with the occasions when the photographer is simply using the camera to compose a scene, or test sound levels as well as subsequently recording.

Monitoring the recording

A most useful feature of almost all video cameras is the ability to view the picture and listen to the sound as it is

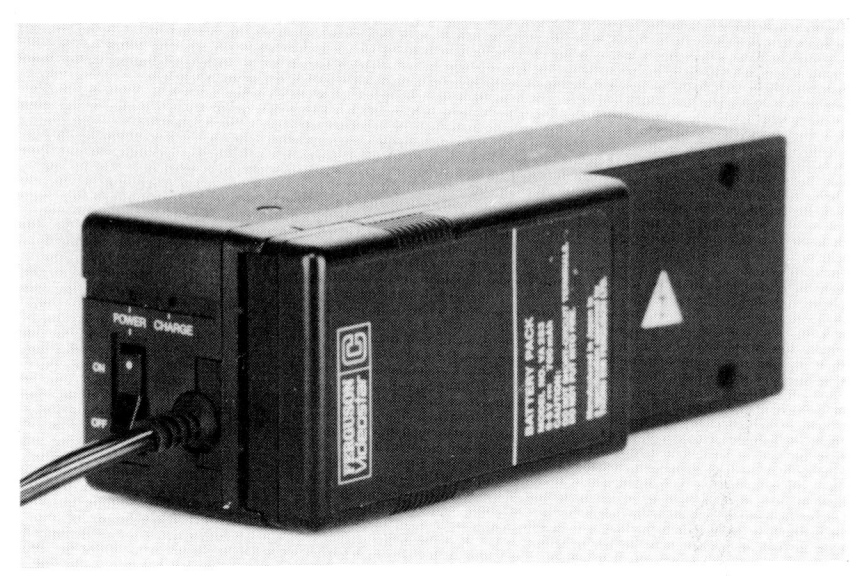

Some manufacturers offer separate battery charging units. These are shown with a variety of typical batteries.

recorded.

Picture monitoring, which is always in black and white unless the camera is plugged into a TV set, is via a very small *monitor* set, viewed through a magnifying lens.

The lens is usually surrounded by a rubber eyepiece and can be adjusted to suit the individual characteristics of each user's eye.

This same monitor can also be used to view a replay of part or all of the recording.

Some camera systems offer a very useful 'review' function where the last few seconds of the most recent recording are replayed just to check the image and sound quality. The monitor also proves to be a useful check of whether the camera is 'live', particularly when in bright ambient light the small indicator lamps on the control buttons cannot be seen clearly.

The location of the eyepiece is important for left-handed operators, as well as for simple comfort.

Many cameras offer a variety of positions for mounting the monitor, and provide the possibility for swivelling it up or sideways to cater for occasions when the camera may be used in a awkward position.

This is a significant consideration when hiring or purchasing a camera system.

Camera-recorder connection

Elsewhere in this book, mention is made of systems that are available either as a camera-recorder combination, called a camcorder, or as a separate camera and recorder joined by a cable.

The camcorder offers a number of advantages not the least of which is that it does not need to have trailing cables attached to some other piece of equipment.

The separate camera and recorder offer a different set of advantages. For example, where the recorder is a normal domestic, mains-powered machine the photographer is forced to stay within range of a mains socket. Essentially it is not a truly portable system.

More frequently the camera is going to be connected to a small portable contained in a pro-

Special Occasion Video Guide

AUTO — FULL AUTO. The indicator AUTO appears when the FULL AUTO button is operated. This remains cancelled

STANDBY. A small white line in the top right-hand corner indicates that the camera is in the record pause mode.

REC — RECORDING The indicator REC appears while recording is in progress.

AGC. When the AGC ↑ indicator appears when automatic gain control is applied during low-light conditions

FILTER. ☼- appears in the viewfinder when the FILTER button is set for natural light.

FILTER. ⌂ appears in the viewfinder when the FILTER button is set for artificial light.

BATTERY — BATTERY WARNING. When the battery power is running low the word BATTERY flashes in the viewfinder.

TAPE — TAPE WARNING. When a tape is loaded which has its safety tab removed, the word TAPE flashes in the viewfinder

Typical displays that might show in the monitor viewfinder on a camcorder.

WHITE — WHITE BALANCE. if WHITE flashes in the top left of the viewfinder. then the white balance needs adjusting. If the indicator does not flash then the white balance setting maintained in the memory is still effective.

M000 — COUNTER The tape counter appears in the viewfinder when DISPLAY-MEMORY button is set for on, and continues to function even when the display is set for off. The M appears when the counter memory facility is selected.

2.9.86 — CALENDAR. The date display appears when the calendar ON/OFF button is pressed Using the SET and POSITION buttons the required date can then be created. Now when you start recording your selected date will be inserted into the bottom left hand corner of the picture.

Camera viewfinder indicators

Various indicators, signalling different modes of operation, appear in the camera viewfinder.

WHITE BALANCE. WHITE(flashing) Adjustment required. WHITE. Previous adjustment still effective, STD. Standard white balance. W-AUTO. Auto white balance

FILTER
☼ Natural lighting
⌂ Artificial lighting

AGC
AGC OFF
AGC ON

W-AUTO

AGC-OFF

To display the camera control settings simply press the MODE INDICATOR button and the information above will appear in the viewfinder.

About Video Equipment

tective case slung from the shoulder.

The recorder will be battery-powered, but have the alternative of mains operation using the supply from a separate TV tuner unit which can be attached to form a total VCR assembly.

This type of unit always uses the standard sized cassettes - ideal where extended photographic sessions are being considered.

It will also often offer the option of separate *video* and sound output sockets, or an *RF (Radio Frequency)* connection suited to the aerial input of a TV set.

A word of explanation is probably needed here. VHS recorders and cameras produce signals representing the image at a frequency and in a form different to normal TV broadcast signals.

In video equipment, the sound and pictures are carried between one recorder and another, or to the TV set, using separate wires -although these may be contained within a single cable sheath.

This is particularly important where you intend dubbing new sound tracks at a later stage, since the picture and sound connections can be easily separated.

To alter the video signal so that it is suitable for connection to the aerial socket of a TV set requires extra processing, which may be done either in the recorder replay circuits, or in an add-on box incorporated in the lead connecting the recorder to the TV set.

Because separate video and sound signals have not had this extra stage of processing, the quality of the final edited film will be improved if the conversion to TV frequencies is avoided when any tape-to-tape transfers are made.

This is particularly important if the video film is to be edited and where several transfers may be needed.

Generally speaking camcorders convert to RF using an external box in the connecting cable - but also offer a video signal cable for tape-to-tape transfers.

Real enthusiasts, anxious to move to near professional

levels using mixing consoles will find some additional notes on this topic in the chapter on post-production techniques.

Which cassette?

Within the VHS format, there are two basic types of cassette in use.

The standard VHS cassette is quite familiar to most people and is used for prerecorded films available from the local video film library or dealer. It is also available in a blank form suitable for use either in a mains powered machine, a battery portable, or some types of VHS camcorder.

The recording or playback time varies from as little as 30 minutes up to 4 hours if the machine is operated at Standard Play speed (SP mode) - or up to 8 hours when the player is used in the Long Play (LP mode).

A second type of VHS cassette has appeared recently. Called the 'Compact' or C-format, it resembles a thicker version of the normal audio cassette and has about the same surface dimensions.

There are some important guidelines to be considered when choosing a tape to be used for video photography. These are dealt with in some detail in the next chapter, but a few general rules are provided here.

First, select a tape made by a well-known manufacturer. **Do not buy on price alone**.

Almost all the tapes you record with a video camera will have to be copied on to other tapes as a natural part of the editing process. Duplicating is also going to be needed to generate extra copies of the final film to send to friends or relatives.

To ensure that copies are as good as possible the original recording should have obtained the very best results possible from the equipment in use.

In the final chapter, there are recommendations and pointers to the best applications for each grade.

The rules applied to the selection of tapes for other formats are much the same as for VHS; however, it should be remembered that there is no compact version of the normal Beta cassette.

3
Cameras Lighting and Sound

Special Occasion Video Guide

Now that you have the necessary grounding, we can get down to specific cases, including the selection of the camera and its accessories.

To an extent, the process of selecting the camera will influence the techniques used in the video film. The features of the more advanced equipment may encourage some kinds of shots that could otherwise be impossible.

Almost all readers will probably select the camera first, learn by trial and error what it can do, and then go on to the planning stage. This is no bad thing, since the camera selection may simply be dictated by what the local rental shop has available.

C-format equipment

Modern VHS camera equipment falls into three main classes. The first, and possibly the simplest to use, are those based on the C-format cassette. They have the advantage of being small and are usually highly automated.

The camera system used in the preparation of this book is illustrated opposite. It typically has most of the conveniences that make it possible for the novice to simply point and shoot, or the more experienced to take over a limited artistic control.

More detailed illustrations show the relatively simple controls of the camcorder. Most easily recognised of the buttons are those which are found on most domestic VCRs. These control the tape transport and include the power ON/OFF, REWIND, FAST FORWARD, STOP, PAUSE and PLAY. Only one of these is used during the recording process: the ON/OFF button!

Two further controls are used for filming, the first is the MONITOR control which is exactly what it says - simply a way of using the viewfinder to compose scenes without providing power to the tape transport.

The second button is a 'one-touch' control which activates the camera and puts it into a standby mode, which is a combination of RECORD and PAUSE.

The second inset shows a convenient thumb-button which, when pressed will start the recording process, and when

Cameras, Lighting and Sound

The C-format VHS camcorder, showing detail of the control buttons.

pressed again will restore the machine to its RECORD-PAUSE status.

There is also a rocker switch marked W and T, indicating the wide angle and telephoto modes of the zoom lens. Pressing on one or other end of the switch causes a small motor to operate to change the focal length of the lens.

The zoom lens can also be manually adjusted, or even set to an extreme position marked MACRO. This has to be a quite deliberate action since the MACRO position is protected by a small detent button on the lens barrel which, when selected, allows macro-photography of very small objects.

Essentially it works as a close-up lens which means that some care is required when it is used, since the focusing has to be precise and the camera mounted on a tripod to avoid movement.

An extremely useful feature of the machine is demonstrated when the controls are left in the RECORD-PAUSE position and the power is turned off. When power is restored, the machine 'remembers' the status it was in and immediately returns to RECORD-PAUSE. Not all cameras do this, so it is useful to check this feature out before getting into any live filming.

One aspect of design which is common to all VHS camcorders, is that even when switched into the RECORD-PAUSE state, the viewfinder monitor continues to work, making it possible to use the time to compose the next scene, without the necessity to fiddle with any more controls!

Located on the side of the camera is a resettable tape counter and a MEMORY button. Using the RESET button returns the tape counter to '000' which may be the beginning of the tape, or simply the point where the next filming session started.

However, the MEMORY button can be pressed at any time and, providing the tape counter is not reset, will 'mark' a point which will stop the tape transport if the FAST FORWARD or REWIND controls are selected.

Of course, if the cassette is removed and then replaced in the machine, the chances are

Cameras, Lighting and Sound

that this function will not work unless re-calibrated with the tape once more.

Adjacent to the counter is the EJECT button. This will only work after the STOP button has been pressed because the tape must be unthreaded from the transport, and returned to the cassette before it can be extracted from the machine.

Just to the left of the REWIND button is a small slide-switch marked LP and SP. This is a new and unusual feature to find on camcorders, although it has existed on home VCRs for some time.

In the SP mode the machine will record and replay the tape at the Standard Play speed, found on VHS machines from their very inception.

In more recent years a Long Play feature has been introduced to home machines, in which the tape runs at half speed and thus lasts twice as long.

Although this may be useful for recording very long programmes from television broadcasts, there are some penalties to be paid which may make it a less desirable feature when using a camera.

This is because there is inevitably a slight reduction in picture quality at LP tape speeds - and a dramatic reduction in the sound quality.

Now, this may not be noticeable when replaying the original recording, but will rapidly become evident when the tape is edited or copied.

Finally, LP recordings cannot be replayed on home machines having only a Standard Play speed. The only solution is to transfer the LP original on to another tape recording in the SP mode.

The three sockets below the tape speed switch are for headphones (very useful to monitor the sound being picked up by the microphone), a cable-linked remote control unit, and a socket enabling the camera to be connected to another VCR, or a television set.

Just below the side of the lens the second level of controls, useful for the more experienced camera operator. The FULL AUTO button sets the electronics of the camera to automatic adjustment for focus, light level and for artificial or

Special Occasion Video Guide

daylight conditions. It is the normal status of the camera when first turned on.

Just above it is the FADER control which allows the scene being recorded to be faded out to a blank screen. Conversely, it can be selected prior to filming to allow a fade-in to be made.

Some camera or camcorder models may offer a choice of blank screen colours, selected elsewhere on the machine.

An important experiment which should be undertaken at an early stage is to check that during picture fades, the sound track also fades with the picture - in some machines it does not!

To the right of the fader control is a very important button labelled BLC. The abbreviation stands for Back Light Control, and is a function that will be needed when the subject being filmed is lit from behind, or where a large part of the background is very bright.

The reason it is needed is because the automatic controls of the camera always use the brightest part of the scene as a reference for the correct exposure. This can mean that the darker parts of the scene are left to look after themselves.

Pressing the BLC button makes the camera a little more sensitive to the darker images, and may solve the problem. More sophisticated cameras offer a graduated control making it possible to exercise an even greater degree of accuracy.

Sometimes it is important to disengage the auto-focusing system, without altering any of the other automated features of the camera. This is the reason for the FOCUS AUTO/MANUAL button - which does just this.

There are several situations where this degree of control may be needed. The most common is where the auto-focus system is unable to make a decision about the correct focusing distance or artistic considerations make it imperative to take manual control.

The differing types of automatic focusing mechanism will determine exactly when it is desirable to select manual methods. For example, ultrasonic sound or infra-red ranging systems will continue to work in the dark.

This may seem an irrelevant advantage but is useful, for example, where the camera is being set up in poor lighting but at the moment of shooting, supplementary illumination is provided.

For the reasons described in the previous chapter, artistic considerations may determine that manual focusing is vital.

Take a situation where the subject of the scene is being filmed across the reception table, framed on one side by a bowl of colourful flowers.

Since the camera user may well be unaware of the region of the picture being used by the auto-focus system, the closer object may or may not affect the behavior of the focusing. Indeed a small movement one way or the other could result in the wrong thing being in focus.

This is obviously a case where manual control is vital, and will ensure that the desired result is obtained. It will enable you to open the shot with the subject sharply focused, and the flowers left

Cameras, Lighting and Sound

out of focus.

Alternatively, you can select to use change of focus to create a point of emphasis. In this case, a fade into a sharp focus on the flowers followed by an artistic change of focus to centre attention on the subject, could add greater emphasis to the scene.

Finally, there is a button marked with small images of the sun and an artificial light.

This is for use when the automatic system for sensing colour temperature is disengaged. It allows the colour filtration to be switched to correct the colour rendition in either artificial light or daylight conditions.

A final control, not shown in either inset, is located on the top of the camera and marked REC REVIEW. Operating it when the camera is in standby, allows a brief review of the final few seconds of the previously recorded scene.

Like almost all cameras and camcorders, our example model is battery powered, using rechargeable packs. In this case the battery packs can have a life of 30 minutes, 60 minutes or 120 minutes continuous recording time.

However, since a fair proportion of the time is spent with the camera on, but not recording, take the quoted times only as a guide of best case conditions.

Since the camera is already fitted with a mono microphone, you may think it unnecessary to invest in further microphones. However, bear in mind this will only be a general purpose type, having all-round sensitivity.

Many cameras allow the integral mic to be removed and an alternative to be fitted either to an accessory shoe on the camera, or perhaps mounted on a separate stand and linked to the camera by cable.

For reasons already described, the prospective video film maker should seriously consider these possibilities. Tests with differing types of microphones will soon demonstrate the advantages.

The monitor viewfinder is a fundamental feature of all good video cameras and provides more than just a view of the scene being recorded.

In all cases it shows extra text or symbolic prompts sent to the monitor by the camera electronics.

These may serve to indicate correct adjustments as well as errors, such as inadequate light, colour balance problems and so on. It also shows when the camera is recording, or perhaps a display of the tape counter to indicate elapsed time or how close you may be to the end of the tape!

Most of these displays will not be recorded on the tape, although in some cases things such as the tape count may be recorded to make subsequent editing processes simpler.

Full size VHS camcorders

Perhaps the most important difference between the camera described above and full-sized VHS camcorders, is simply the size of the machine and the extra recording time that becomes available when using full-sized VHS cassettes.

However, the larger size may also offer more space to pack in extra features currently unavailable on the C-format

Cameras, Lighting and Sound

cameras although this may change as more and more C-format camcorders appear in the market.

Nevertheless, the basic principles of the smaller cameras are repeated in the larger versions and so we will avoid going over them again. Instead, let us take a brief look at some of the extra features that may be offered.

Looking at the camcorder shown here, you will see that the main controls are mostly the same as for the smaller camera discussed earlier.

However, it does have some extra features which can add extra dimensions to your production - or even make the unit very useful for simple editing of the sound track.

First, the microphone is of a stereophonic type. This means that left and right channels are recorded, making it possible to replay the tape through mains VCRs and TV sets having stereo capability.

It also means that when remote microphones are used in place of the unit attached to the camcorder, a stereo type will

A full-sized VHS camcorder showing the controls in close-up in the inset picture.

Special Occasion Video Guide

have to be selected.

Another feature to do with sound is the *AUDIODUB* button which permits the subsequent recording of a new sound-track after the original recording has been completed. It does mean that the original sound track is wiped off and a new track substituted, but on occasions this can be an advantage.

However, there are a few things which might appear confusing and unfamiliar.

The WHITE BALANCE button is used when the automatic assessment of the colour temperature of the light illuminating the scene is switched off. It simply enables the user to switch the filtration to correct colour balance for scenes lit with different kinds of artificial light.

The iris is a means of controlling the amount of light passing into the camera. In the version shown here, automatic control of the iris can be switched off by pressing the plus or minus buttons. When the scene is lit with a marginal amount of light , pressing the plus button gives more sensitivity to the camera. Pressing the minus button will cut the amount of light, eventually causing the picture to fade out to a blank screen.

Automatic operation of the iris is returned to the camera by pressing the IRIS-STD button.

More controlled fade-in or fade-out is given by the button marked FADER.

The third control, marked AGC, may be used to override the automatic exposure setting process of the electronics. It could be operated, for example, to produce special lighting effects.

Typically, with the camera in auto-mode and pointing say, at a sunset, the AGC button would be pressed to avoid the exposure setting being altered as the camera is panned away from the sunset.

It is a control that requires some experiment, before being used in earnest, and may well add some extra artistry to the scene being recorded.

One final point before we move on to examine the last type of camera system you might encounter.

Cameras, Lighting and Sound

Clearly the full-sized cassette has forced an increase in the size of the camcorder. This means it will normally be supported by the shoulder during filming.

A substantial tripod will also be an asset when using a camera of any size. Surprisingly, it is even more important when using the lighter small cameras, than with the larger and heavier versions.

The reason for this is probably that the normal small amount of handshake we all suffer from - and which is most likely to occur when a telephoto lens is being used - remains undamped because of the lack of weight.

In addition, smaller size does not permit a shoulder rest to be built into the design.
Even though the full-sized camcorder has weight and can be held more steadily when extreme telephoto shots are being made, a shoulder support or tripod is still a real boon.

Camera-recorder combinations

The final type of system you may be offered in a rental shop or perhaps consider buying, is the three-unit combination of a video camera, a separate portable full-sized cassette VCR which would be carried on a shoulder strap, and a TV tuner unit.

This is an all-purpose system, which may well be considered by more serious enthusiasts, who want to keep the cost of purchasing video equipment to reasonable limits.

An illustration on the following page shows the complete system. The TV tuner pack is mains powered and would normally be permanently installed at home.

It provides the functions of the tuner sections of a mains-powered VCR. This means that all the usual TV channel buttons, plus timer controls are provided.

It is connected between the TV aerial and the television set and, when coupled to the VCR forms a complete unit which operates just like a normal domestic machine.

Often it also supplies the power for recharging the battery packs, needed when the VCR is used as a portable.

The recorder, when used

Special Occasion Video Guide

This is a three part video system comprising video camera, recorder and a tuner.

separately from the tuner, is usually powered exclusively by battery packs. It is fitted with the normal set of tape transport controls, but has extra features not found on camcorders.

For example, it may offer limited editing facilities such as AUDIO DUB, where an existing sound track can be replaced with another one from a hi-fi system, another video recorder, or perhaps from a microphone. This is done without disturbance to the existing pictures.

The PICTURE INSERT control provides a way of adding new scenes to a recording without causing a massive disturbance to the picture quality at the point between existing material and the new recording. Naturally, the new recording will also erase anything after the insert point, up to the end of the extra scene.

Like camcorders, portable VCRs normally cannot be connected directly to the aerial socket of a television set.

Conversion to TV frequencies has to be done either by a cabled adaptor powered by the VCR, or more normally by circuits inside the tuner section of the VCR system.

This means that extra sockets are to be found on a portable VCR, which may not be found on a camcorder.

Because the camera used with this three-part system is a separate unit, it is often much smaller and lighter than a camcorder.

Nevertheless, it controls the portable VCR in the same way as if the two were a single entity. It has the standard thumb actuated button for recording, plus automatic white balance, AGC, fade, back-light adjustment and manual overrides to the auto features.

The real virtue of the camera-VCR-tuner combination is that it combines the best of a home mains-powered VCR, with the convenience of a portable camera and recorder.

It may be the perfect solution where the cost of buying a camcorder in addition to retaining the home VCR, is a little too much for your bank manager's comfort!

Advanced camera systems

One of the advantages offered by the VHS tape format is that a very wide range of camera systems are now to be found in retail shops. Indeed, the real enthusiast can even find products which very closely approach professional standards.

However, in the same way that a novice should avoid selecting a complex 35mm still camera when a disc film camera would be adequate, an attempt should be made to match the video camera system to your experience.

The examples of equipment shown here are ideal for anyone from the beginner to the relatively experienced camera user. You can go further, but you will almost certainly have to buy the equipment rather than hire it!

Selecting the tape

It may seem at first sight that it is a little superfluous making a careful selection of the type of tape to be used when planning a video film. Not so!

Most stockists of tape seem to make a big thing out of price while offering little advice on why manufacturers produce such a variety of grades of tape.

This is a pity, since each grade of tape is formulated to bring specific advantages to certain applications.

For example, tapes recorded when making a video film with a camcorder will usually be copied during editing and often once again to make duplicates of the finished results for friends and relatives.

It is a natural and unavoidable consequence that picture and sound quality always deteriorate a little each time another generation is added to the copying process.

When the original has been made using the highest grade tape available, this deterioration can be reduced to a point where it may be unnoticeable - at least for the first two generations of copies!

However, if the tape is of a more pedestrian type suited to day-to-day recording of TV programmes and never normally used for making duplicates, quality problems may well show up quite quickly in the copies.

Interestingly a new type of tape has also appeared primarily directed at users of video recorders offering hi-fi sound quality.

These are normally mains powered, home-use VCRs which can be connected to a hi-fi system and will often allow a simulcast to be recorded with a superb sound track.

A simulcast, by the way, is where a TV station broadcasts the pictures from a concert, while a stereo radio station offers a simultaneous VHF sound broadcast. The VCR can take a feed from both sources and records both the high quality radio sound and the normal sound which accompanies the television pictures.

Video recorders of the normal type will replay the standard TV soundtrack, but machines fitted with the hi-fi option can be switched to replay the alternative, and much higher quality hi-fi soundtrack.

Recording in the hi-fi mode places considerable demands on tapes and requires a grade of sufficient quality to permit the extra information to be recorded without any undesirable side-effects.

Generally, the best rule-of-thumb to apply when buying a tape for use with a camcorder or portable, is to go for the highest grade. Take any opportunity to discuss the projected application for the tape with a dealer.

Lights and accessories

As for ordinary film cameras, the amount and type of light needed to obtain correct results from a video camera is very important. This can be an acute problem when making a video record of a wedding, since much of the recording will take place inside a building.

The first shots may be in the bride or groom's house, followed by extensive recording in a church, registry office, or other building designated for the ceremony, and then finally at the reception.

Fortunately, few people are married in the evening, so there should be plenty of light outside, but whether it penetrates the buildings will depend upon the available

Special Occasion Video Guide

window light.

Typically, most good video cameras will produce acceptable results in modern houses where windows are large, but poor results will often occur if the light source, such as a window, is included in the shot.

This is because the contrast between the lighting of the exterior scene (or even the net curtains) is much higher than that of the people being filmed inside the room.

As already explained, the camera circuits may decide to set the iris to correctly expose the window scene, leaving the intended subjects looking too dark. Some compensation is possible using the BLC control on the camera, but usually it is a situation best avoided.

Churches are more of a problem particularly if they are old, or fitted with stained glass windows. In the latter case two things might happen. If there is enough light, the recorded scene may be badly affected by the colour of the window glass. This is very difficult, if not impossible to cure using the camera controls alone.

Worse still, there simply will not be enough light to make a good recording. It may be that the monitor shows a reasonable black and white image, suggesting conditions are favourable, but this is not a reliable indication. It is true that modern video camera technology allows some cameras to record without problem in surprisingly low light levels.

Nevertheless, it is always possible that some interiors are still not well enough illuminated. The previous visits to the church and reception rooms may have been on a bright day, whereas the wedding may take place in overcast conditions.

This is where the video film maker should seriously consider the possibility of supplementary lighting. A little basic knowledge of correct lighting techniques may also be an advantage.

First, avoid using the direct light from powerful quartz halogen lights attached to the camera itself. These produce poor results - partly because the people being filmed can never look at you for fear of being dazzled.

More importantly a single source fitted to the camera produces a very unflattering light, often accompanied by unsightly shadows which will always be in the worst place!

Ideally, the best form of simple lighting arrangement will comprise two lamps either of differing power, or placed at differing distances from the subject. The main lamp should be set at about forty-five degrees to the subject and at the closer distance.

Choose a distance which ensures the whole area of the scene is evenly covered. Next, place a fill-in light in line with the camera, to relieve the depth of shadowing from the main light.

One way of relieving the direct and powerful effects of a quartz halogen film light is to diffuse the beam with some thin white cloth on a wire frame made from a coathanger, and placed a foot or so in front of the light.

Such lighting arrangements are most suitable where the subject being filmed is relatively static, but is are obviously impractical in any more animated situation.

Where the subjects move, or the camera has to remain free and mobile, bouncing the lights from light coloured walls or the ceiling may provide a solution.

However, the idea should be applied with caution. Beware of coloured walls which can tint the illumination falling on the subject giving them a quite unexpected skin colouring!

Special Occasion Video Guide

In the post-ceremony activity, a stepladder will be an advantage, taking you above the crowd to capture scenes such as this.

4
Planning for a Wedding Shoot

Special Occasion Video Guide

The success of any video film relies on two basic elements. The first of these is a well planned succession of shots which can be assembled into a coherent documentary of the event.

The second element is added in post-production stages, but should be planned for from the beginning. It is the essential contribution brought by a first class sound-track and good titling.

This chapter uses the detailed planning of the wedding film shot during the preparation of this book as a typical example.

The documentary as a record

Many of the video films made by amateurs are documentaries. This is because fictional story-lines for a video require a director, script, actors and a host of other elements that severely complicate the task.

Nevertheless, this does not absolve the video camera user from planning - even if the proposed video record is nothing more than a 'snapshot' movie of a holiday.

Indeed, it is the powerful discipline imposed by the nature of the still camera that forces the user to concentrate on isolated key events. A novice video camera user is thus often poorly 'trained' to consider the more important element of continuity that arises from attempting to make a video film. All too often, the appearance of the finished result may give the feeling that much has been missed.

As a rule of thumb, record each scene leaving yourself with the impression that the camera is running for too long!

However, long before the camera is picked up, careful preparation will ensure that the final production will become a treasured addition to the memorabilia of the new family.

So, what are the elements of a good documentary - and how can these be adopted in filming a wedding?

All films will need a title and an endpiece. Both will be in the form of text which can be either specially produced by an artistic hand, or may be adapted from something already printed.

Planning for a Wedding Shoot

Typically, this might be an invitation, part of a reception menu - or even an announcement of the forthcoming event in the local newspaper.

Between these two text-based shots will be the film itself which logically must also have a beginning, a middle and an end.

This is where some difference of opinion could conceivably arise between the bride and groom, and the film-maker.

Where you may consider that the arrival of the bride at the church is the best starting point for the film, those who see the film afterwards may be disappointed that some of the preparations leading to the wedding have not been included.

For the happy couple, the wedding day starts with waking up. But, with the exception of the groom, for whom the memory of having to deal with a hangover may be a humorous recollection, it may hardly be the starting point for a good film.

Some time spent with the

A horse-drawn carriage makes a memorable high point in any wedding video.

family well before the wedding day will help to establish just when the filming should commence.

Bearing in mind that there is normally only one video camera, it has to be decided whether to attempt to record the preparations prior to leaving for the church - and if so, which of the principal 'actors' should be filmed.

Coupled to this should be the thought that, whereas scenes of the groom's preparations might be more amusing, the often frantic process evolving at the bride's home may well provide more interesting material.

Typically, the bride will go through the stages of hair-styling, make-up, and dressing. Of course, discretion will have to be exercised and some scenes left unrecorded to avoid embarrassment.

Against the theme of the bride's preparations there will be a natural background of high points which could include the general hubbub of tradesmen delivering last-minute accessories and gifts, brides-maids and perhaps pageboys arriving and wanting to help,

together with the inevitable suppressed panic of the bride's parents.

Although this may appear a very complicated series of events to film, you can take comfort that at least everyone will be moving forward to the same timetable. This is vital to the film-maker who also has to remember that the very next sequence of shots will take place some distance away at the church.

As explained in the first chapter, notes in the form of a timetable will be a valuable aide-memoire as well as providing the basis for deciding what can or cannot be filmed.

In the case of Mr and Mrs Reece, whose wedding is featured in

Father and bride leaving for the church in style!

this book, an outline of the film was easily started by learning that the bride was to travel from home to the church in a horse-drawn carriage.

Clearly, this dictated that the early scenes had to be shot at the bride's home. Also, since the carriage was horse-drawn, it made it possible to record her departure, together with a minute or so's travelling down the road waving to neighbours and still get to the church ahead of her by car.
Now a horse-drawn carriage is a fairly unusual form of transport for the bride. Not all film makers will be so fortunate in having time in hand to reach the church by virtue of faster transport.

Indeed, there is always the hazard of getting stuck in a traffic jam not experienced by your subjects!

The time of the bride's arrival at church will always be dictated by the vicar - given the sort of leeway often allowed for her to be traditionally late.

Using a rehearsal, the journey from home to church can be easily checked out, making allowances for any differences in traffic loading or transport used on the actual day.

This will help you to determine whether or not you can risk leaving your own departure for the church until the last moment.

An early chat with the vicar will save considerable pain and problems. Some do not like film makers and photographers working in the church during the ceremony. Others allow this, but set limitations on the areas of the church or parts of the ceremony that can be recorded.

In addition, the vicar may prove a mine of information on the spots most often used for the wedding pictures.

Because the still pictures will remain the most important official record of the day, there is very little chance that you will be able to rearrange scenes to suit the making of the video film.

Indeed, there can be significant advantages in having the professional photographer remain the centre of everyone's interest.

Extra 'candid camera' shots

Special Occasion Video Guide

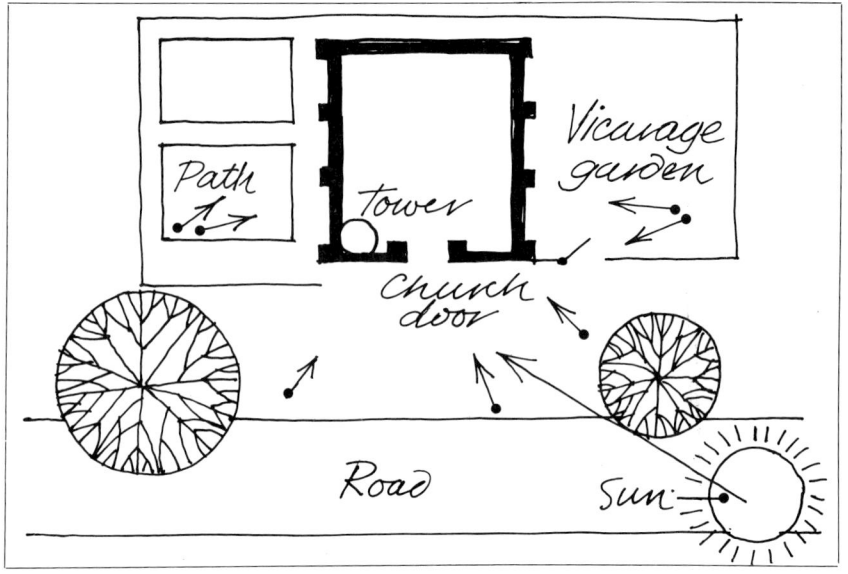

[Diagram: A plan-sketch showing a church layout with labels: Path, Tower, Vicarage garden, church door, Road, Sun, with trees and arrows indicating camera positions.]

This plan-sketch was made to give simple diagrammatic notes of the position of the sun and several suitable camera locations that may subsequently be used.

taken during the arrangement of a wedding group will usually produce the moments that every photographer treasures - a totally un-selfconscious subject.

Another useful bonus likely to come from the presence of an official photographer is the current desire for much more artistic pictures rather than a straight photograph for the album.

This now leads many photographers to take much more time and care in arranging their subject - giving more time for the film maker to get into position and start filming.

While you are at the church prior to the wedding, make sketches and notes of suitable filming locations and in particular note the direction of any prevailing lighting.

This is obviously more important outside since shooting against the light may be a very difficult and sometimes impossible task. It will at least avoid you planning to take up a camera position which could cause technical difficulties on the day.

Planning for a Wedding Shoot

Inside the church, you may well encounter problems of insufficient lighting.

Determining exactly how much light is needed is tricky at the best of times. The shrewd film maker will take the camera along on the preview visit and shoot some test shots to make absolutely certain that conditions are suitable.

In addition to checking on the amount of light available, it is also important to assess the predominant colour temperature of the light. Although the chart shown in the previous chapter gives a guide of what may be expected, the only real assurance will be obtained by making trial shots well before the day.

If it is possible to see what happens if the available daylight is affected by clouds do so, since this may be very important where the interior is predominantly lit by daylight through clear windows.

Where this might be the case in many chapels or modern churches, older churches often have stained glass windows, rendering the available light totally unsuitable for anything except special fill-in shots of attractive lighting effects that may be produced.

For example, sunlight through a stained glass window might make it worthwhile to record the the pools of coloured light thrown on the floor. These could be used during post-production as an artistic link between one scene and the next.

The real problem with churches having stained glass is the lack of light. Since the artificial lights already installed in the church are not designed for a video film maker, there may well be insufficient for good pictures.

The only alternatives in such a case are either to give up the idea of recording inside the church (especially if the vicar doesn't like the idea of extra lighting), or to find a way of making up the deficiency.

The simplest solution might be to persuade the vicar to let you install brighter bulbs in the existing lights if practical: the light fittings may be inaccessible other than by long ladder.

Another alternative is to consider portable battery-powered, or semi-portable mains-powered lighting.

This will undoubtedly need extra planning, a willing assistant to set up the equipment, and a rehearsal to test both colour temperature effects and the modelling the light gives to the faces of the subjects being filmed.

The last-hope alternative is a single battery powered film light carried by an assistant. But even here, practice will be needed to ensure the assistant is trained to follow the direction of the camera and also ensure the light is pointing in the right place.

Wherever you are forced to use artificial lighting, it is vital to make tests prior to the event to learn its limitations and advantages.

After the ceremony

The same guidelines outlined above and used to create the plan for filming up to and including the scenes immediately after the wedding ceremony, can equally be applied to the planning of scenes shot at the subsequent reception.

Is there enough time for you and your assistant to travel from church to reception to film the arrival of the couple and their preparations to receive the guests?

What is the layout of the reception room, and the best positions to film the key events?

Is there enough available light, or is artificial lighting needed?

Resolving these matters is essential if you are to stand a chance of making a really good film.

The end product of the experiments, rehearsals, note-taking and sketches should then provide a good basis for the next stage - which is to make the film itself.

Don't forget the sound-track!

Unlike the pictures made by a still photographer, video equipment is also capable of recording a sound-track.

The final quality of the track will be dependant on three basic factors. The first of these is the quality and type of video recording equipment used.

Perfect examples of the problems of lighting: there was sunshine on the day the wedding shoot was planned (top left), but the day itself was dull. Catching the bridal couple leaving the church is a vital sequence, important enough to warrant some form of external lighting in the porch area if conditions are as gloomy as here. Left: Even sunshine can pose problems, if as here it is dappled and giving strong contrasts of light and shade. It is worth practising filming in those conditions and you could also end up with some useful fill-in shots.

Top left: Do persuade the caterers to locate key scenes at the reception for your benefit not theirs. Here the cake-cutting is marred by strong foreground shadow, inadequate background lighting and overhead foliage which could easily creep into shot.
Top right: Don't film the 'white' bride against a white background light, all of which can confuse the camera's light assessment, resulting in the foreground figures being rendered as silhouettes.
Centre: Do make sure that you have a tactful 'minder' with you to keep others out of your 'sight line', especially relatives and friends anxious to get their own pictures.
Bottom: Do check your backgrounds: this attractive tracking shot has been ruined by the noticeboard and signs. With permission from the relevant authorities, these could so easily have been removed.

Planning for a Wedding Shoot

Most machines only record a monophonic sound-track. A smaller number offer the possibility of going further and recording stereo - some even going so far as to record what is known as hi-fi sound, in addition to the standard sound-tracks.

Finally, a few 8mm video recorder systems also offer monophonic sound recorded digitally through the *PCM* or *Pulse Code Modulation* system.

In a chapter which is primarily about planning the video film itself, it may seem irrelevant which recording system is employed by the equipment.

However, the significance will become clearer as we consider the second factor affecting the quality of the sound-track.

It is simply the type and location of the microphone used with the recorder.

The position of the camera and recorder system is going to be largely dictated by the need to obtain good pictures without becoming intrusive. The best location to achieve this is invariably not the best place for the microphone.

Microphones are normally provided as an attachment on the camera. It might be a useful location if the only shots you plan are close-ups of your subjects, but is certainly not the best place when longer range shots are needed.

It is important to bear in mind that the further you are away from the sound you want to record, the more chance the wanted sound will become confused by ambient noises originating from other sources.

As the third factor which determines the ultimate sound quality, consideration must be given to these unwanted sounds.

The type of microphone often mounted on a camera.

Special Occasion Video Guide

For example, are any of the prime locations under the flight path to an airport? Or perhaps there is a busy road very close. If so, will it be behind the camera or in front?

Are there any other major sources of noise which might be avoided - and if so, where are they?

Finally, we cannot afford to forget some extra sounds which might be essential to the success of the film, but which originate from directions other than the one the camera is pointing in.

Typically, and most often, these will be the church bells and the organ. The vicar will certainly know if either or both are being used.

Running over the factors that affect sound quality will help you to come to a few decisions about the equipment that will be needed on the day, and any special provisions that might have to be made.

Take the question of the video recording system being used: if it is monophonic, then simple mono microphones can be used.

If the recorder can record stereo sound-tracks, then it will be fitted with a standard stereo microphone. If this is exchanged for types having a more directional sensitivity, make sure they are also stereo.

In the case of recorders offering a specially high-quality hi-fi sound track, the microphones will be quite good enough, but you will need to to ensure their location is such that they pick up the best sound possible.

The preceding chapter explained how microphone placement, or the selection of directional models helps to ensure good results. If part of your plan is to record some of the scenes using a separate microphone on a stand, add this note to your equipment list for the day.

Wild sound-tracks

Good though a video sound-track can be, it does suffer from one major disadvantage which will not be noticeable until all the shots are assembled into a single film.

Unlike the professional material we see on television, the sound recording ends precisely at the time vision recording stopped! Hardly

Planning for a Wedding Shoot

surprising, but quite irritating when trying to make something with professional polish.

Professional films are usually shot using two separate machines. One records the sound and the other the picture. Each of them can be started and stopped independantly of the other.

In addition, film makers will often use sound from other sources, added to the main sound-track during post-production.

Despite the rather large gap between the features of a domestic video system and the sort of thing found in a broadcasting environment, it is possible to use the same ideas in your own video film efforts.

It might occur to you to add commercially recorded material to the film later, but this carries some important legal consequences, since almost all records are subject to copyright and cannot be used without the risk of subsequent prosecution!

A simpler and perhaps more useful alternative is to record a wild sound track using a separate tape or cassette recorder.

It does mean yet another piece of equipment to lug around and set up on the day, but the benefits will far outweigh the disadvantages.

A good film gains from elements of continuity which may be provided visually. However, this often means two or more cameras, or perhaps a series of scenes which can be set up, recorded and linked under the guidance of a director and continuity assistant.

An alternative which is easier for the documentary film maker is the wild sound-track which can be subsequently dubbed on to the edited version of the tape, either as a substitute for the original sound-track, or perhaps as a background supplement to the existing one.

The beauty of the wild sound-track is that the recorder could be set up to record, say, the organ, or the church bells and just left to run by itself.

It can also provide a continuous recording of the ceremony, including the responses of the bride and groom which will help to cover over the gaps

Special Occasion Video Guide

that naturally occur between one shot and the next.

One very useful alternative to an audio recorder, was employed when filming Mr and Mrs Reece's wedding. In this case, I had no audio recorder handy, but did happen to have two of the cameras illustrated in this book.

Consulting the vicar, I first found out where the bride and groom would stand for most of the wedding. I then arranged a microphone having moderately directional properties on a stand very close by.

This was connected to the second camera, tripod-mounted and located to one side of the church. The lens was preset and focused to ensure that, as the couple stood at the right point, it viewed both of them and even took in a side view of the vicar!

This camera - using a standard VHS E180 cassette - was set running before the bride entered the church, and only stopped as the couple left.

Naturally, since the camera was unmanned, the only interesting scenes recorded visually were those when the bride and groom stood on the spot appointed by the vicar. This lasted no more than five or ten minutes.

Nevertheless, the sound-track, recorded on a microphone ideally placed for that part of the ceremony, could then be used in place of the sound recorded on the mobile camera which was being used to obtain various shots from behind the couple.

There is one snag, however. If it is your intention to use a great deal of the wild sound-track then it is unlikely that there will be sufficient pictures recorded to make the two match!

This is where fill-in shots of architectural features of the church, or perhaps the patterns formed on the floor by the light from the windows and recorded during rehearsals, will come in handy to make up for the shortfall.

Such extra material can be introduced during the post-production phases of the film.

Once again, experiments made during rehearsals are useful to gain experience but may also prove a valuable source of additional material for use in the finished film.

Notes, plans and storyboard

There have been many mentions of the necessity for notes and sketches during the planning stages of your video film. However, apart from the generalised and fairly basic examples given in the first chapter, you may have some difficulty deciding exactly how these can be assembled.

From the first meeting with the bride and groom, or perhaps with parents, you should try to collect enough information to make two lists.

One of these will simply be a list of the equipment and materials needed during the day.

The second is a timetable setting out where you will have to be at each stage to prepare for, or actually record scenes of the film. An extract from both of these is illustrated.

Two other invaluable items are the diagrammatic plans of the key locations for filming and, if necessary, storyboard sketches of the formal and predictable

Planning for a Wedding Shoot

parts of the day, to act as a guide to the way the lens should be adjusted, or the camera panned.

Although a short storyboard was constructed for Mr and Mrs Reece's wedding, it only dealt with the church ceremony and gives some indication of the difficulties of providing variety to a series of scenes of the back and side of the couple.

In some cases, it may be possible to get in front of the couple, and behind the vicar, but bearing in mind the necessity to avoid disturbance, and the time it takes to move from one camera position to another, regretfully this idea may have to be abandoned.

Another alternative is to post yourself in the choir stalls, in front of the couple, before the bride and father come up the aisle. In many church weddings the couple and their family will retire to the vestry to sign the register and this might be the right moment to move down the church to the door, putting you in position to film the wedding procession down the aisle.

Decisions like this are best made after studying the

Special Occasion Video Guide

geography of the church, talking to the vicar, and discussing the preferences of the bridal couple several days prior to the wedding.

Incidental and fill shots

It cannot be too strongly emphasised that incidental and fill shots will be absolutely vital to the success of the final production.

There are several reasons for this. Repeatedly filming the backs of a congregation from different viewpoints while they are singing hymns can rapidly induce monotony.

By using a wild sound-track of the singing to provide some continuity, fill-in shots of the church architecture - or even introducing still pictures of the couple as children, taken from the family album, will help to provide a little extra interest.

Similarly, incidental shots of the guests or family while waiting for a scheduled event to occur will also add considerable value to the record.

A wedding is an occasion when many people meet either for the first time, or perhaps for the first time in many years. The video film will provide a first-class souvenir of these happy encounters for the recipients of copies of the recording.

Covering up mistakes

Unfortunately, mistakes can happen no matter how much preparation is undertaken.

Sometimes, the mistakes will not be yours but those of the guests, the couple or the family. That is one occasion where it may be wise to be sensitive to those you have filmed and censor the recording!

The more serious problems occur either because something that should have been recorded has not, or a technical error occurred in handling the equipment, spoiling an important shot.

Sometimes a recovery can be made by persuading the participants to repeat something privately afterwards. But it is not always possible to secure such cooperation, so the film maker has to resort to a cover-up to hide the shortcoming.

Planning for a Wedding Shoot

Take a typical situation, one where the camera view gets blocked in the melee outside the church. It could have been avoided by standing on a short step-ladder placed by your assistant, but possibly this was forgotten.

It is one of the rare occasions where you can speak to those in your way while the camera is running. It means that your voice will be on the sound track, but this is less important than getting the vital shot.

If it is undesirable for your voice to remain on the recording in the final version of the film, it can be can be covered up in postproduction by adding sound from alternative sources.

Perhaps these might be recordings of voices off-camera, made at an earlier moment, or even something selected from a commercial record.

The sort of things that can be useful are from sound-effects discs that have recordings of unidentifiable crowd noises, church bells, and a selection of many other sounds.

In a case where a scene has been completely missed, be prepared to film directly from colour still pictures.

However, this is a technique which should be used sparingly, as your error would soon become obvious to the film's final audience.

Use your ingenuity!

Keeping your wits around you and making use of ingenious devices during filming may be a way of solving difficult problems. It can even help to add your own artistic stamp to the film. Reflecting surfaces can sometimes be a boon to the observant film maker. For example, a mirror on the wall of the reception room can be used to get round an obstruction to record a vital scene.

When using such tricks, it is important to make it obvious to the viewer what you have done.

Mirrors reverse an image from left to right. Unless you give some clues that the picture is shot via a mirror, the viewer may wonder what on earth has happened to his or her eyes! Reveal your technique by zooming from a wide angle view showing the frame, to the wanted reflection of the subject. Similarly, the reflections in a pool of water, or a lake, can provide a useful and rather

Special Occasion Video Guide

attractive point to start a camera pan, lifting up from the reflection to the real scene.

Transitions from one shot to the next can be given more continuity by using things and people to 'point' to the location of your next scene.

This is dealt with in much more detail in the next chapter, but here are a couple of ideas to set your imagination at work.

A profile of a group all looking in the same direction could be usefully linked to the following shot of the activity they are observing.

A panned shot of a bird in flight from the church roof, flying down to land on the path outside the door, can become a prelude to the following shot of the couple leaving the church.

Take a careful look at the way in which professional directors add drama, humour or interest when linking one shot to another. When making your own film, adaptation of these ideas is often easier than you might suppose.

Plain windows in a church give enough light on a good day for the camera to operate without the addition of extra lighting.

5
The Elements of Camera Technique

Special Occasion Video Guide

Before we get down to the work to be done on the wedding day, let us take a short look at some of the important elements of good filming technique that will ensure the post-production is a relatively simple task.

The importance of ensuring continuity in the film has already been emphasised, and a few of the things that make this possible have been described.

Wild sound-track, for instance, has been stressed as an important aid to being able to string scenes together. After all, every time you stop the camera to move to a new position, the accompanying sound-track will normally also be interrupted.

If the camera is swung from one direction to another, the attached microphone points with it. This can be a disadvantage if you wish to record the picture in one direction and the sound from another.

An example of this kind of situation is in the church where you may move to film the congregation, while needing to continue recording the voice of the vicar, who is perhaps in a totally different direction.

The wild sound-track which can be recorded from a choice of one or two fixed microphones gets around this problem, since it can be dubbed onto the recording during post-production.

Although sound may be an important way of linking scenes, the most important connection that can be made is by visual devices.

Everything you do with the camera should have some point. It should provide a 'vehicle' by which the viewer is taken from one shot to the next.

Professional film makers have lots of ways of doing this, including dissolves, fades, cuts, panning, zooming and dollying. But what exactly do these terms mean - and how can they be effectively applied by the amateur?

The language of the camera

Essentially, the camera, when used properly, can become an extension of the viewer's eyes. In the hands of a a good film maker, it may also trigger

The Elements of Camera Technique

emotional responses which will help the audience feel they are actually there.

Alfred Hitchcock was a past master at this kind of thing. Scenes in some of his films have almost nothing happening on the sound-track, but we still seem to become one of the cast in the drama, through the way the camera is used.

If you like, the camera is also a storyteller and sometimes a participant in the plot. It uses a sort of language to set the scene, and raise the level of impact on the viewer.

What follows is a sort of a lexicon that will help to develop your own ideas on how the wedding story can be told.

Panning: This is probably one of the most widely-used motion picture jargon words, and one of those best understood by the lay person. It describes a movement of the camera sideways, or up and down, while it is actually recording a scene.

In a way, it is the one device that most closely follows what we do with our eyes. As we turn our heads to concentrate attention on something of interest, the direction of the camera can be similarly altered to take the viewer from one interesting action to another.

Its real virtue is that the connection between one view and the next is continuous. Thus, in theory, it is a perfect scene-to-scene linking device.

However, it can go wrong!

In the two sketches shown on page 76 the camera commences by showing a close up of the profile of a person looking to the right.

Suddenly, something happens behind the subject, and the camera is panned left to take it in.

The viewer can find this a bit disturbing because it would seem more logical to pan right, to examine what the subject is looking at!
In another situation, a shot may open with a signpost showing the name of the church, but the camera pans in the opposite direction to reveal the bride's carriage approaching the camera.

Here, the viewer has a timing

Special Occasion Video Guide

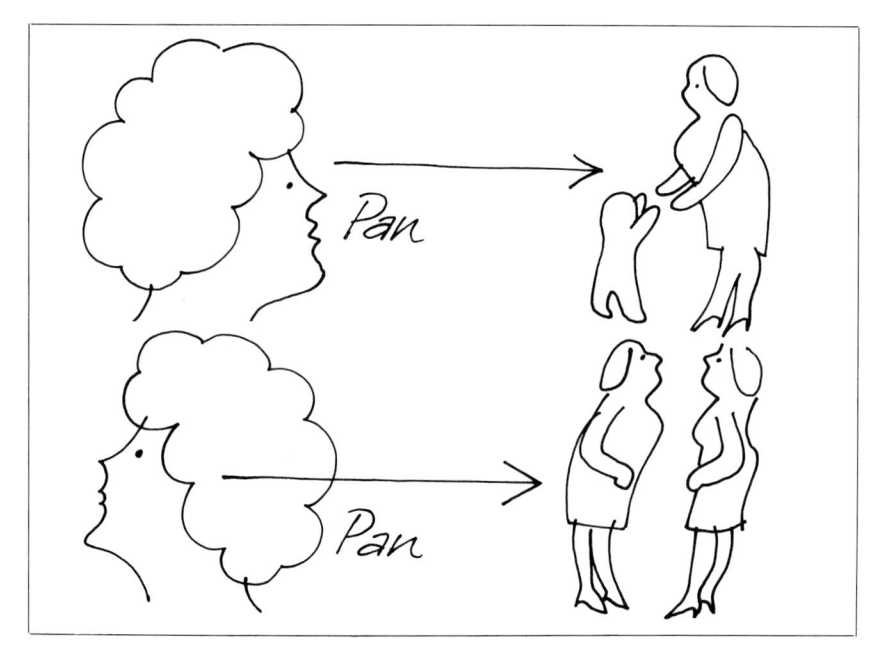

A pan should follow naturally from the eye, as in the top sketch, and not awkwardly from the back of the head as in the bottom drawing.

point of reference. It is clearly *before* the wedding rather than afterwards.

Thus the camera pan can be used to add emphasis, either in drawing the viewer in directions they already want to go, or to establish some point of reference.

The speed of the movement is also of great importance and, because of technical limitations, has some strange side-effects. Try this out in a test and it will be very easy to see why.

Nevertheless, a really fast pan sweeping from one view to another can be used to gain dramatic effect, even the feeling of speed.

Conversely, the slow pan allows the viewer to take in the detail of the scene being surveyed. Essentially he or she is being told 'Look at this, isn't it beautiful!'

The Cut is where two scenes follow each other, but clearly with a difference in the time or the location between the two scenes.

The Elements of Camera Technique

Because you have only one camera, many of the shots you will make during the wedding day will be linked by a cut.

However, this can be a very hazardous way to assemble a film because, unlike a professional film unit, the time difference between one shot and the next will always be there.

In the professional situation, the presence of two cameras makes it possible to cut smoothly from one to the other without a time gap.

If the majority of your film consists of a sequence of shots always directly cutting one to the other, the viewer might get the feeling that the whole thing is a kind of moving album of still pictures.

The cure is to apply common sense and use a variety of 'tricks' to cover up the technical limitations of your equipment. Make sure that where a cut is made from one shot to the next, the time interval is small between the two, and try to cover the break with a continuous sound-track from the wild-sound recorder.

If it is impossible to do this, some other form of visual link will be needed to convey the impression of the passage of time.

Fade: This is where the fade will be immensely valuable. Whenever a scene is faded to a blank screen, it is as if the storyteller (that is you!) has ended a chapter of the story.

The next scene is like a fresh start which may occur in a totally different place or at a very different time.

Some video cameras allow you to fade to a coloured screen. This can be a useful emphasis which may add something to your story. But watch that the emphasis you add by using a fade to colour is the right one!

Say that you are filming the departure of the happy couple as they leave the church. The road their car is using appears to be very busy and, as it enters the traffic stream, you decide to fade to a blank red screen.

This can leave the viewer a little disturbed - it may appear the film maker is suggesting the couple are driving into danger!

The same scene, faded to a restful green, and then

Special Occasion Video Guide

followed with an opening shot of the green gardens of the reception rooms is a much more satisfactory device.

Fading into a shot can have an equally useful, though totally different effect on the viewer.

It can convey the passage of time since the last shot, but may also be used to ease the viewer into a dramatic change in the pace of the film.

You might decide to end the scenes at the church with a shot of the sun-lit bell tower accompanied by the a satisfactorily noisy peal from the bell-ringers.

Logically, the next scene will be of the bride and groom arriving at the reception rooms and passing a few quiet words with each other before the guests arrive.

Although the contrast can be given dramatic effect by using a cut from the previous shot, the viewer may feel more happy if the camera fades in on a close-up of the couple followed by an expansion of the picture to show the new location.

Dolly: Strictly speaking this is nothing more than a camera platform on wheels. It was a very popular and almost essential device for early film makers.

The dolly provides a useful way of moving the camera from one place to another as smoothly as possible.

In the days before zoom lenses, it was a method of following action from one point to another or perhaps concentrating the viewer's attention on one part of a scene.

Although it is easy to assume that with modern cameras the zoom lens can be a substitute for the dolly, this is not so. As you will see shortly, the zoom lens is used for very different purposes.

Few amateurs will want to go to the extent of making or buying a dolly of the type used by professionals, but it is possible to obtain a very good substitute which can be employed on smooth floor surfaces. It is a tripod fitted with wheels.

An alternative, one to be used with care, is an open motor car. Filming from a moving car is difficult because of the need to keep the camera steady - and this may call for an inordinately skilful driver.

Nevertheless, it is an excellent way of providing a link from say, the scenes at the church, to the scenes at the reception. Try filming the couple's car or carriage from your own.

Sometimes, when desperation sets in, you can make yourself into a human dolly. The camera can be moved from one point to another simply by walking with it!

However, to do this while keeping your subjects in shot, avoiding undue camera shake, and preventing yourself tripping over unseen obstacles, needs audacity and skill.

Some people can actually film with both eyes open, using one for the viewfinder and the other to see where they are going. Very clever if you can do it but it does need practice!

Zoom: This marvel of modern optical technology is really a way of combining an infinite number of camera lenses into one. It makes it possible to shift from wide angle, to normal or telephoto effects, without changing the lens.

Almost all video cameras can zoom, changing the focal length of the lens either by motor drive, or manually.

In a camera with lenses of fixed focal length (in other words, just like the lenses in our eyes) the magnification of the scene is only altered by changing lenses during a break in filming.

We human beings have to use binoculars or telescopes to achieve a similar result.

With a zoom lens it is possible to smoothly change the magnification of the scene while actually filming.

Because we cannot use our eyes in the same way, it lends a feeling of artificiality to the scene.

This is why, as a general rule of thumb, one should avoid zooming while the camera is running.

This is not to say that one should never use zoom - it can sometimes be very effective but the moment should be chosen with care.

Video magazine writers have coined the word 'hosepiping' to

Special Occasion Video Guide

describe the indiscriminate way in which a camera is zoomed in on a central point of the scene and then zoomed back out again.

If zoom is used, it should be applied in the same way that italics lend emphasis to a particular word in a piece of text printed in an otherwise normal typeface. In other words, with discretion to avoid repetition.

A typical example of the value of zoom would be in establishing the setting for a particular scene in your film. The scene could open showing a pleasant panoramic view of the churchyard and then, using a combination of panning and zooming, take the viewer to a close view of the bride and her father arriving at the church.

Like dollying, using the zoom lens while filming takes practice - but of a different kind. Pressing the zoom button is easier than moving a dolly but skill is needed in appreciating how the results will be seen when incorporated into a full film.

Note how rarely the zoom was used by professional camera operators during the wedding of Prince Andrew and Sarah Ferguson. Also, observe how zoom lenses may be useful at sporting events but are rarely used in a documentary film.

Focus: Since most modern video cameras are fitted with autofocusing devices, it may seem rather odd to be talking about the use of focus as a filmatic device.

However, there are plenty of occasions where taking manual control of focusing is more than a mere technical necessity.

Rather in the same way that the travelling shot obtained from a car or a dolly can be a way of linking one point of the filmed activity to the next, differential focus can play a part in adding emphasis to the filmed result.

Camera lenses of all types have difficulty in focusing sharply over a wide range of distances. In the case of modern video cameras, this may not be very obvious, except where the difference in the distance of the nearest object and the farthest one is great.

It will be also more noticeable if the closest object is very close to the camera.

This fact can be employed when the camera is viewing the wanted subject through a 'frame' formed by some much closer object. Changing the focus from the closer object to the more distant one, without altering the camera position can create a effective artistic impact.

Similarly, deliberately moving from in-focus to out-of-focus, or vice-versa can be used as the end or starting point of a shot, making the cut to the next scene a little more gentle.

Once again, though, this device needs to be used with care in case the meaning you intend is misinterpreted by the viewer.

Imagine the effect on the viewer as the scene closes with a shot of somebody drinking from a glass and then going out of focus. It might imply that the film maker is suggesting the subject is about to pass out from too much drink!

Using camera technique

In that section of your film where you have plotted your actions using a storyboard, it is possible to include notes reminding you which of the above techniques can be logically applied, and when.

Elsewhere, you will not be able to make such definite plans, largely because you will be filming totally unscripted events. In such a case, it is wise to keep at least a skeletal idea in your head of which shots are likely to act as real 'scene' or 'act' changes in the film.

These are the points where 'emphatic' techniques such as the fade, or the use of focus changes, can provide just the link that will make a smooth and logical flow possible when finally assembling the film.

There is one last idea which may be employed if you really want to produce a purely cinematic impact on your audience.

Even though your video film will have sound, why not try adding the kind of subtitles that were used as a substitute for dialogue in silent movies?

Obviously, these will have to be added in post-production - but they are simple to insert between shots and add a touch of personal humour which may be appreciated by your audience.

Special Occasion Video Guide

Clearly, you will not be able to apply subtitles as done on television i.e. as a footnote to the picture running above, but this adds to the effect.

If one live shot cuts to a subtitle and then to the next shot, it gives the humorous impression of watching a silent movie - and might also cover up for a missing scene!

6
The Great Day!

Special Occasion Video Guide

By the time the dawn breaks on the great day, you should have completed a detailed series of planning steps, and selected and tested the equipment to be used.

You should even have some preliminary 'atmosphere' shots already recorded for the final post-production.

As weddings are an event that cannot be repeated for the camera, it is well worth checking through every piece of equipment to make sure that it is working before you leave home.

The battery packs for the camera system and the wild-sound recorder must be fully charged and, apart from a brief test to make certain no faults have developed, they should not be used until you arrive at the location selected as the starting point for filming.

Check you have enough tape and, ideally, that it is fresh from the pack. Most weddings will take no more than one and a half hours of recording time, though it is unwise to rely on just one E180 cassette in case accidents happen.

Something that is easily overlooked and yet is absolutely important is the necessity to acclimatise the tapes you will be using. Simply this means unwrapping them at the beginning of the day and allowing them to re-adjust to the temperature of the locations you intend using for recording. The same should be done for the recorder.

The reason for this is because abrupt changes of temperature can often be accompanied by the formation of condensation on the surface of the tape, or in the path of the tape transport inside the camera.

When this happens, damage can occur to either the tape or the camera or, at the very least, the tape will not pass smoothly through the recorder and the film will suffer disastrous effects.

Label the cassettes in some way so that you know in which sequence they are to be used. It may not seem important to do this while they are still unrecorded, but it could save untold problems later.

During the pressures of filming small details like this can easily be overlooked.

The Great Day!

If you have additional microphones and a portable sound recorder, remember to pack extra batteries and audio cassettes.

Record brief sound tests with each microphone to check the recorder, the microphones, and the connecting leads that will be used.

Similarly, if portable lighting is to be used, check that the batteries are charged and that you either have a spare bulb with the kit, or access to one. Even go so far as to test the lamps before packing them.

Finally, tick everything off against your equipment list and be sure you include the plan diagrams, notes and any storyboard you have made as part of the preparations. A notebook for on-the-spot jottings will also prove useful.

Your assistant - essential when making a good video film - should be thoroughly briefed on the connection of each piece of equipment. If necessary, give information on how to operate lights and the sound equipment.

From here on in the job might look as if everything is under control, but do not forget weddings always produce a few surprises: that is what makes them such a fun family event!

It may be that all this is beginning to sound complicated and too much to cope with and that you are beginning to panic a little about your debut as a film maker.

Don't worry: if you have gone through all the stages described in the earlier chapters of this book you can be sure that both you and your assistant will rise to the occasion without major problems occurring.

Keeping to the plan

The problem with all the plans you have laid is the unpredictable event lurking in the background. The most important is the weather. Is it comparable with the weather you experienced when making trial recordings and tests at the key locations for the film?

You might consider that if the weather is better than during the rehearsals, you have an advantage. But bright sun can bring a few problems of its own: perhaps awkward contrasts of

Special Occasion Video Guide

light and shadow in the church and reception rooms.

By the way, have you packed an umbrella? An enormous golfing brolly can be useful in all sorts of situations - from covering you and your assistant if it rains to providing shade on the camera lens if you have to shoot into the light.

But it is now time to move off to the first location, or perhaps to the places where some preparations are needed.

For Mr and Mrs Reece's wedding, the first call was at the church to set up the wild sound recorder and its microphone. (In this case, you will remember, the wild sound was recorded by a fixed and unmanned camera.)

A quick check was then made of where the first guests had seated themselves. There is nothing so annoying as choosing what seems to be an ideal camera location in the planning stage only to find the view is obscured by a guest unexpectedly sitting at the back of the church!

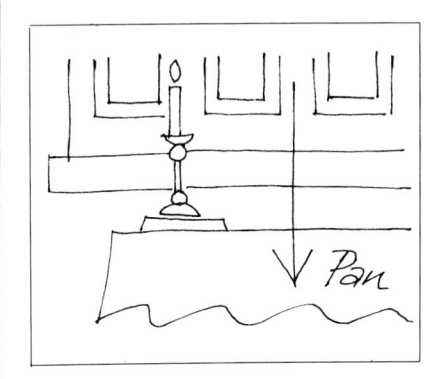

These three storyboard sketches show useful shots and techniques that may be used later to link other scenes

A final discussion with the vicar will help to ensure that the extension leads for the

The Great Day!

microphone and the microphone itself are in a safe place.

Should you decide to use a second unmanned camera, you may be able to get the vicar to stand in the position he intends using, then focus and set the camera so that at the right moment in the ceremony the couple will be correctly framed.

Finally, start to film incidental shots, which can be used later during post-production.

A few ideas for fill-ins

Set your camera on a tripod in the centre aisle of the church and focus on the stained glass windows over the altar, or any other convenient and pretty architectural detail.

Start shooting and slowly pan the camera down to reveal the place where the couple will eventually stand; then rapidly swing the camera round at least 180 degrees, pressing the pause button before you stop panning the camera.

The rapid swing will result in a colourful blur on the screen and the shot may be of use cut into a shot, filmed much later, of the

Further examples of atmosphere shots that may be used in the edited production.

87

bride and her father entering the church.

Flowers in a stand by the pulpit make a good incidental insert. Again, using the tripod and the telephoto end of the camera's zoom range, get a close-up of one of the blooms and then zoom back without moving the camera to show more of the church itself.

Try to hand-operate the zoom as the change of focal length can be done much more slowly.

You might be in real luck if one of the church ladies is still arranging flowers around the church. Get some shots of her working away, as these can provide a useful scene to set the mood of your audience during the early stages of the video film.

Go outside the church, to the door from which the happy couple will emerge. Check the steps or path to see if there is any confetti still lying around from a previous ceremony. If there is, scatter some on the church steps (make sure this is not against the vicar's rules) and select a suitable place and angle from which to get a close-up.

Start your shot by filming the empty doorway - it will not matter if the doors are closed. Take in the whole doorway and then pan down to the steps, finally zooming in on the confetti. Hold the close-up for at least one minute.

This sequence might prove very useful as the closing scene of your film, with the close-up as the background to an END title superimposed during post-production.

Read your notes, storyboard and plans to see if you have scheduled any other atmosphere scenes in addition to those just suggested.

Try to remember the need to use fade and differential focus as ways to avoid straight cuts. It will be easier to do this with incidental shots than when shooting the unscripted parts of the day.

By the time all this is done, it will be getting close to the time for you to leave for the bride or groom's home. Here, you will be filming on the run, so to speak, as there is no formal sequence for the family to follow.

However, before leaving the

The Great Day!

church, arrange that your assistant switches on the wild sound recorder when the organ starts playing. Even though it may commence well before the arrival of the bride the music will form a valuable recording which can be used in post-production.

When you go to the bride's house, make sure you film incidental sequences, such as the closed front door, before you knock and go inside. These again, may be very useful when assembling the finished film.

Filming inside a house can produce quite a number of technical problems - unless you switch the camera to purely automatic function. That way focusing, and adjustment to the variable light levels will be taken care of, just leaving you to select the right focal length for the lens (usually wide-angle), and correctly frame the shot.

However, one difficulty more likely to be encountered here, rather than at the church or reception rooms is the direction of the lighting.

If you are relying on available light coming through the windows, it is important to position most of your shots so that you are beside a window rather than risking the possibility that one of your subjects may pass in front of it.

If you are unlucky enough to end up in the situation where a person you are filming gets between you and the prevailing light source, it will be vital to make adjustments for this, using the back-light (BLC) control button on the camera.

With so much activity going on, you may experience difficulty in deciding when to stop. In such a case, don't! You will have more than enough tape and, hopefully, battery capacity to shoot with impunity.

However, when you think the action may be irrelevant, keep the camera running even when you remove your eye from the eyepiece. That way, you will have a continuous sound-track, your subjects will relax, but you will still be ready to film the unexpected.

The fact that the camera will be recording a blank wall, the floor or anything it happens to point at, is of no importance since the sound-track may be the more valuable thing. Poor

Special Occasion Video Guide

pictures can always be edited out.

When the car or carriage arrives, go outside and film incidental shots of the horses and groom, or the radiator, bonnet and attached ribbons, and other details of the car.

The departure to the church is a delightful thing to include in your film, but you will have to ensure that you can still get there before the principals.

There are two ways to record the departure of the bride or groom for the church. One technique is to follow them out of the house, continually shooting while on the move.

If you are a novice, it is inadvisable to attempt the professional camera operator's ploy and precede the group, walking backwards to keep them in view. It is a very dangerous and difficult excercise to undertake!

An alternative is to go ahead of the bride and her father, taking up a position about half-way down the front garden and to one side of the path they will walk down.

This way, you can pan to follow

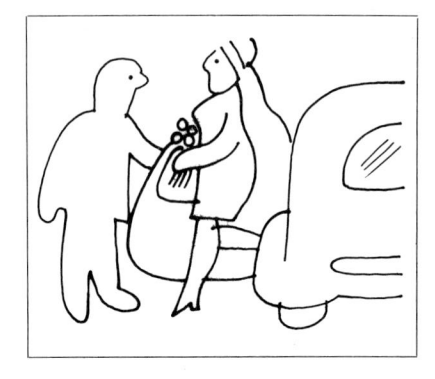

Top left: Film a long shot of the bridal car approaching. Top right: Allow it to fill the frame as it comes closer. Bottom left: Make sure you are the 'right' side of the car door as the bride climbs out. Bottom right: Now get into position for a long shot of the bride and her father.

them out into the road.

When they reach the car, if needed, tell them to wait until you are in position to take a shot of them getting in and driving off.

With correct timing, you should be back at the church well ahead of the bride, which might even involve riding pillion on a motorcycle. This will give you a chance to film the arrival of late guests, perhaps including the groom, the best man, the bridesmaids, church, almost every move of the principals in your film can be predicted.

Start by filming a long shot of the bridal vehicle approaching from as great a distance as possible. By using a long shot, which means filming with the lens set at about mid focal length, the viewer's anticipation can be heightened.

As quickly as possible, cut after about thirty seconds of recording, and change the focal length of the lens so that you open up the next shot with a telephoto view where the vehicle fills the viewfinder. In many cases, this shot can then be held until it arrives at the church.

You should make sure you are already in a position where the camera view is not obstructed by the car or carriage door being opened, thus offering a clear view of the bride getting out.

You can then rapidly move to the church doorway to film father and daughter walking up the church path to the porch.

Try to avoid close-ups if only because the bride might have a

and the bride's mother.

If the wild sound recorder has not yet been switched on, make sure this is done since there will be no time to attend to this detail later.

Recording the ceremony

Filming the arrival of the bride and her father at the church will usually be a straightforward and simple operation. Indeed from this point until the moment the bride and groom leave the

Special Occasion Video Guide

veil which will make it difficult to see her face, until she gets in the shade of the doorway.

At this point there is bound to be a pause while the vicar welcomes father and daughter and time is spent making the last-minute adjustments to the bride's gown.

This can usefully be used to enable you to move inside the church to the position you have selected to film the walk up the aisle to the choir steps. If you have positioned yourself close to the aisle, select a fairly wide-angled view so that you do not have to zoom out to a wider focal length when the bride passes you.

It is almost certain the bride and groom will exchange meaningful glances when they meet at the choir steps and this is a moment that you should be in a position to capture if at all possible.

Your storyboard should now take over, since this will help you to remember exactly what is needed on the recording. In addition, you will have had plenty of opportunity to discuss your plans with the key participants and they will

know what to expect when you are spotted moving around the church.

At the same time, because the planning will have been detailed, your assistant should be able to operate alone without having to get instructions on the next move to be made.

This is a very important point since at the end of the ceremony, as the couple are disappearing through the church door, your assistant should be dismantling and packing any gear and taking it out to the transport, ready to move quickly to the reception.

The final scene inside the church will be the wedding procession down the aisle. Your best position will be just inside the church doors, in line with the aisle.

Thus, using a slight telephoto focal length, you can get a full length picture of the couple coming down the choir steps into the nave, and then gently zoom back to a wider angle view to encompass the guests on either side of the aisle.

The shot can then be cut, followed by a quick move

outside, to film the couple emerging and the guests circulating round them, offering their first congratulations.

This will also probably be the last scene on your storyboard because events outside the church tend to become hectic until the wedding photographer takes charge to set up the group photographs.

Sometimes, though, the church precincts are unsuitable for this and photographs are left to be taken in the grounds of the reception rooms.

However, wherever the wedding pictures are taken, it is a golden opportunity to film the guests and family. By now they are feeling relaxed and happy and there will probably be many meetings of old family friends and relatives which will be worth filming.

It can even be rather fun to include the wedding photographer in shot: the problems experienced in marshalling people into a wedding group can produce some amusing scenes.

Indeed, keep your camera running, even when not using the eyepiece. Once again, the

The Great Day!

sound-track will be useful, and the less you have to fiddle with technical bits and pieces the more you will merge into the background.

All the time keep an eye on the progress of the couple towards the vehicle taking them to the reception. This is where it will be most difficult for you to get clear shots of their departure. It is also the point where all the guests want to throw their bags of rice and confetti!

It is probably the one occasion when a short set of steps will prove useful. Get them set up in a prime position to take in all the action, post yourself ahead of the crowd and keep the camera running until the vehicle has cleared the well-wishers.

The reception
Now it is time to run or get back on your bike! Getting to the reception ahead of the main body of guests can be very useful since the first event you will probably want to film is the bride and groom welcoming their hungry and thirsty guests.

But, before you get to the point of recording once again, take a moment to check the camera

Special Occasion Video Guide

Key scenes at the reception: speeches, toasts and of course, the cutting of the cake.

batteries and the tape remaining. They may need to be changed for a new pack, and this is a good moment to do it.

If there is a decent opportunity, use the waiting time to usefully film incidental shots of the wedding cake, the buffet (if there is one), and the wine waiters and waitresses

carrying and handing out the drinks.

Naturally, if somebody is popping champagne corks, try to get a good shot of this as well.

While all this is going on, get your assistant to set up the wild-sound recorder and

The Great Day!

microphone near the place selected for all the speeches.

It can be quite useful to tape your extension camera microphone, or the wild-sound recorder mic to the same stand used by the reception rooms' own microphone.

Start the second tape machine recording, and keep it running for at least thirty minutes, finally turning it off when the speeches are due to start.

At the same time, you may find it worthwhile to change the camera microphone for one having more directional properties. This is because the selective properties of a hyper-cardioid microphone will allow it to capture less of the hubbub of sound coming from outside the field of view of the camera.

Once everyone is seated and the food has begun to circulate, you should then revert to your storyboard. Check out the selected camera locations to make sure the speeches can be easily filmed and, if possible, rig the camera on a tripod ready for this event.

You will certainly find it easier to handle and keep steady - a particularly important factor when recording people speaking formally.

The toasts are best filmed in longer shot, so that the person proposing the toast and the guests are in view at the same time.

However, the reading of the telegrams is usually a moment to switch between close-ups of the best man's face, and longer shots of the laughing guests or the newly-weds.

The visual gap that will arise from switching shots between the two viewpoints can be masked when assembling the film by clever sound dubbing from the wild sound tape.

The penultimate scripted event on your storyboard will be the cutting of the cake. Make sure you have reserved a good position, probably next to the wedding photographer.

Finally, you will want to record the farewells of the happy couple as they leave the reception to go on honeymoon. Hopefully, this will not be after dark, but if it is, you will need your assistant to handle a single portable

Special Occasion Video Guide

filming light and its battery pack.

Work as a team and remembering the earlier warning about the effects of such lighting, your assistant should try to ensure the light remains on one side of the couple, no matter from what angle you are recording the scene.

This is where prior rehearsals, even if they took place in your own back garden several days before, will ensure a smooth-running sequence of filming.

Finally, try to remember to end the shot of the disappearing car with a fade. If the vehicle has been 'adorned' with tin cans and old shoes in the traditional manner, this will make for a humorous close. It will make the subsequent editing of the video film so much easier. It will also add some artistic impact, putting a full stop at the end of the last 'sentence' in your film.

Do ensure you can move freely behind the couple as they mingle with guests after the ceremony, and try to capture as many smiling faces as you can — no one will want to be left out of the final film.

Do get as much informality as possible in your filming: remember, most of the 'still' pictures will be posed, so yours should be animated. It also helps to be at the church sufficiently in advance of the ceremony to capture, for example, the groom, best man and attendants (below). Chances are you will not be able to gather them together like this afterwards.

7
Post-production Preparations

Special Occasion Video Guide

Post-production is the process applied to a series of recorded scenes, destined to eventually make up a complete video film.

It is the technique of assembling and editing them into a coherent unit and also involves the addition of title sequences and changes or adjustments to the recorded sound-track.

Just as the location filming required careful pre-planning, selection and preparation of equipment, post-production demands the same kind of attention to detail if the end product is to be truly successful.

Above all, do not think that because you made a successful series of shots of the wedding, that you already have a video film fit for duplication and distribution among friends and relatives.

For a start, there will be parts of your recording that are deliberately or accidentally faulty. Also, the sound-track will almost certainly want tidying up, and the whole thing still lacks titles!

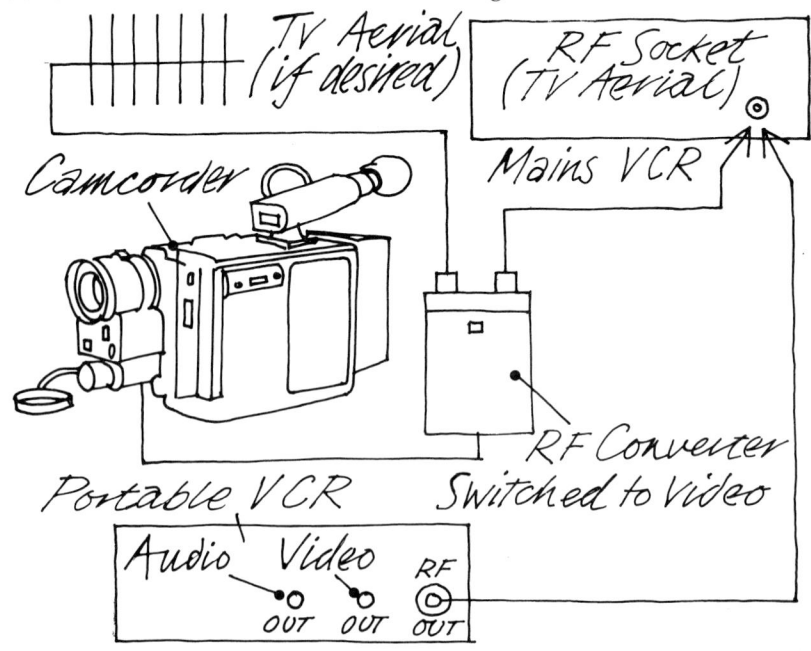

The simplest connection for editing uses RF leads to join the equipment together. The lead from the camcorder contains an RF converter tuned to Channel 36.

Selecting the equipment - the simplest set-up

In this chapter, we are concerned with the task of assembling the equipment that will be needed, connecting it together and making careful tests before commencing the real job of finishing our video film.

There are several levels of complexity of post-production equipment. Choosing which suits your own needs and abilities is largely up to you. Essentially, the more you are prepared to spend, the better chance you have to add still more polish to the recording.

Possibly you have a domestic mains powered video recorder, but it will need careful examination to see if it is suitable for editing your video film.

All picture editing processes require the process of duplication to be adapted to allow a series of shots arranged in any order on the original tape to be rearranged in a new order on a second tape.

Two types of recorder facilities make the task considerably easier to avoid obvious 'joins' between sections originally recorded on different tapes, or at different places on the original tape.

These are called *assembly editing* and *insert editing*. Simply, assembly editing enables one sequence to be added to the previous one, without visible defects in the finished result. Insert editing is a way of inserting a new sequence in place of one that has already been recorded on the tape.

Normally, if this process is attempted without insert editing functions available on the recorder, dire visual effects will occur at the points where the new joins the old.

At its very simplest editing involves connecting the portable recorder, or the camcorder, to a second machine, which itself is connected to a TV set.

All VCRs will allow this to be done, but sometimes you will find you are limited to working at TV frequencies. This means that any of the cables used to connect the VCR to the TV may be used to connect the two VCRs.

The signal coming out of the

Special Occasion Video Guide

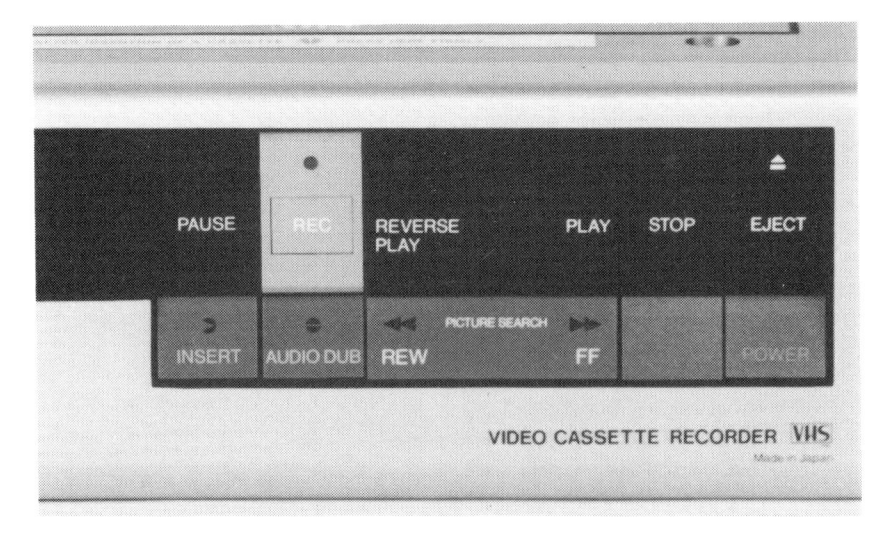

portable or camcorder is just like the signal coming from a TV station and can be tuned to a spare channel and selected the same way as one might tune BBC1 or ITV for instance.

Although this type of interconnection will work, it is far from the best way to achieve good quality pictures on the finished version of the videotape.

Here is a basic specification for the features of a domestic VCR which represents the minimum for best results. It should have separate video and sound sockets; be able to audio-dub; and be fitted with an electronic pause control.

Electronic control is much preferable to the early mechanical lever controls which required a very firm touch to make anything happen.

Extra features which will prove very useful are video insert, hi-fi sound (plus a control for adjusting the sound recording level), still frame, and fast picture search.

A typical portable VCR which has many of these features is shown here.

Audio connections for this type of machine are usually the standard DIN type of multi-pin plug and socket where it is

This sort of VCR is useful as a master recording machine when editing. Note the useful control functions.

Post-production Preparations

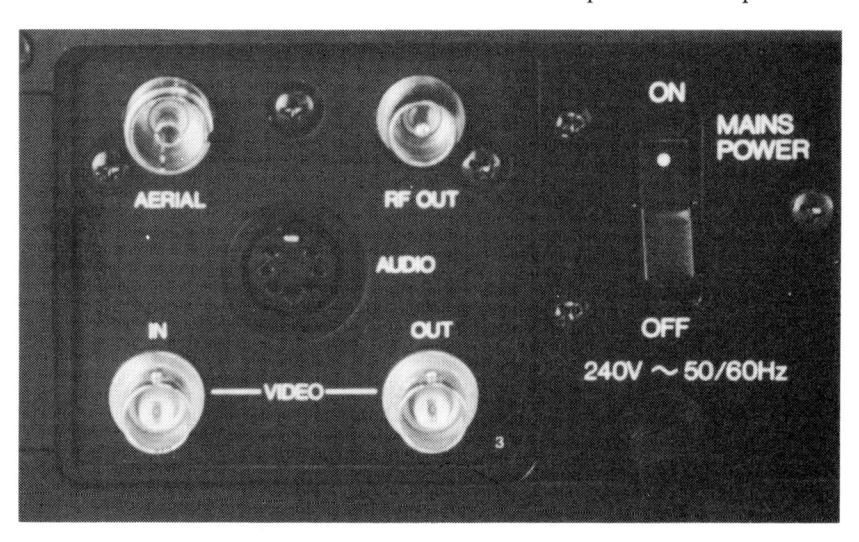

from a European manufacturer, or the simple single-pin phono connector if it comes from a Japanese source.

An important feature of the type of plug-and-socket used for video signals is that most often they use what is known as a BNC connector. It looks a little like a coaxial aerial plug but has a bayonet fitting which locks the connection in place.

Some video recorders, instead of having separate video and sound sockets at the back, are fitted with a multi-way connector, commonly called a SCART socket. The name is acquired from the international

The rear panel of the VCR shown above. Two connections are possible to other devices, one at video using BNC connectors, the other at RF using coaxial plugs.

The SCART socket found on some of the latest types of VCR requires the special lead shown, to permit connection with a hi-fi system.

standard which defines which pin connection is used for what.

The SCART socket is very useful, since it carries video-in and video-out, as well as mono or stereo sound in and out of the machine. Using the correct combination of leads (easily obtained from good local radio and TV shops), connections can be made to suit the most complex of editing arrangements.

Extra items which will be very useful are a tripod for the camera, some type of transfer lettering, such as Letraset or Blick to make up titles, a notepad to keep editing notes together, the leads to connect the equipment and some stiff,

coloured card in a selection of pastel shades.

The card size need be no bigger than a standard A4 sheet of paper, but should be reasonably strong and have a smooth, unglazed surface.

The lettering you use should have a range of capital letters which are 10mm or so in height. This is equivalent to the printers size scale of 36 points. Try to choose a typeface that suits the occasion and is also not too difficult to apply.

Typically, any script typeface - something that looks like beautiful handwriting is very difficult to use. Arranging letters so that they are in a

An editing console with a small titling camera and card holder mounted on the top.

Post-production Preparations

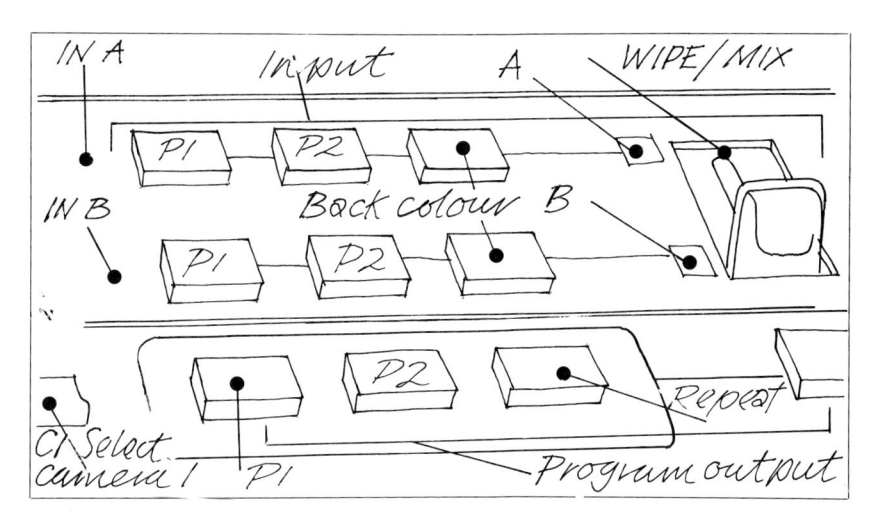

[Diagram of editing console with labels: IN A, Input, A, WIPE/MIX, P1, P2, Back colour, B, IN B, P1, P2, P2, Repeat, C1 Select camera 1, P1, Program output]

straight line is made problematic because the letters have such a curved shape.

The more rectangular and bulky lettering so often found in stationers is very legible and easy to use, but suffers from being less visually pleasing.

Probably one of the easiest and most suitable typefaces is one that looks like the print of this book page. It might be an advantage to select the italicised form for some of the lines of text to make them stand out.

Advanced equipment

For the more ambitious, there is a variety of equipment available for purchase but unfortunately not generally available for short-term hire.

It offers the possibility of taking the post-production process to almost professional levels. If you do not intend going this far you may skip this section and move to the next.

Typical examples of the type of equipment referred to are illustrated on this page.

The first, and very useful item is the editing console which, in the case of the example shown, permits three cameras and one VCR to feed signals into the console, and one VCR and a

This editing console can wipe or dissolve mix between any two cameras. There are some problems in doing the same between two VCRs.

103

monitor to be connected to check and record the output results.

Note that since all the picture signals passing through this console are at video frequencies, the type of connector used is BNC, and not the normal coaxial sort used for the aerial socket of the TV set.

One of the cameras which might be used is the very small accessory camera shown on top of the editing console. It is primarily designed for recording titles and captions which are arranged on the stand at the left end of the console.

The lens is specially designed to focus accurately over this short distance and the whole arrangement has the merit that the size of the picture area is precisely determined on the plastic support sheet which holds the title card.

The console will also control the sound-track independently of the pictures and for this reason offers connections for a separate microphone or line input.

An odd connector on the back of the console may cause a great deal of puzzlement to many. It is labelled *'black burst'* and in simple terms it is a synchronising signal originated by the console and used when more than one camera is plugged into the mixer at the same time.

Normally, each camera times the starting point of its picture scan, using its own internal circuits. This timing is then passed onto the VCR as part of the video signal and so no conflict arises.

However, where more than one camera is used, each could conceivably commence its frame scan at a different moment to the next and so, when mixing from one to the other, the VCR gets in a muddle and the transition is accompanied by picture noise and jitter.

By providing a black burst signal from the editing console all the cameras are forced to run synchronously with each other to avoid the problem. In some cases the signal is fed via the multi-way camera cable, but in others a separate connection may have to be used.

At the camera, the black burst lead will probably have to be connected to a socket called GEN LOCK. This is an

Post-production Preparations

Throwing the confetti as bride and groom leave the church or registry office — authorities permitting — will provide you will a colourful and happy sequence, shots which could prove useful, say, at the end of the film as well as in their proper chronological sequence.

abbreviation for Generator Lock, indicating that signals arriving via this input will take over the responsibility for locking the camera timing to the other equipment being used.

However, editing our wedding video will not involve this sort of complexity, and so the facility can be neglected for the moment.

The front control panel offers two methods of mixing from one scene to another, using either a horizontal or vertical wipe, or a simple dissolve mix.

The only time this will be useful for our wedding film is where the title camera is being used to add captions, titles, or to 'lift' a picture from a still colour photograph.

Making your video film titles

The start and end of your video film will be considerably enhanced by the addition of a title and an end-caption.

Earlier, it was suggested that a blank invitation card be saved as it might become suitable for use as a title. Before committing yourself to using this, try setting up a camera and recorder, focused on the card, to see if the lettering is large enough and of the right colours to reproduce well when recorded.

Some types of printing will not look good when filmed, particularly if the lettering is silver on a white card.

If it turns out that you have to make your own caption cards, by far the simplest and most professional looking method is to use a transfer lettering method.

Of course, if you or a friend or relative have outstanding artistic abilities, it might be possible to design and produce something special.

Whatever the technique, try to avoid using a pure white background for the text. Instead go for a suitable pastel shade, or even cream. Similarly, if the captions are hand-produced, avoid dense pure colours like bright red, blue or green.

These do not reproduce well in copy tapes when the original recording has been duplicated.

Post-production Preparations

Transfer lettering comes in a vast range of styles and typefaces, but it is important to choose one that is sympathetic to the subject.

Special Occasion Video Guide

The lettering at the top has been applied out of alignment and will obviously mar the finished production, no matter how professional the filming. The second example illustrates the kind of typeface which is wholly inappropriate for the subject — it is much to heavy. However, the third example is both well-chosen and well-applied.

Ending the film with a suitable caption will present some interesting problems - not the least in selecting suitable wording. You may think, for example, that the use of the bald words 'THE END' is not good enough.

If the 'star performers' have a sense of humour, you could close on a still-shot of a babyware shop, accompanied by a caption such as 'the shape of things to come'. But be sure that this is something they do look forward to before attempting to use the idea.

Whatever the choice, use the same rules as suggested for the title. It is useful to appreciate that a lot of words on the screen does not work very well, so keep all captions down to a minimum.

The dimensions of the caption cards are important because the area occupied by the text should correspond to the ratio of the screen dimensions.

These are 1.33 :1 which means the width of the text area should be 1.33 times the height from its top to bottom. Typically, a card could be made up with the text confined to a space which is 12mm wide by 9mm deep.

If you choose a larger size of paper, then the lettering should be scaled up to suit. It is not a good idea to use a much smaller dimension than 36 points (10mm) mentioned earlier. Whatever the text area you choose, always make sure the card is larger, giving some space to clip it to a holder while the recording is being made.

Illuminate your titles with even and diffused daylight wherever possible. It will avoid the possibility of problems arising from colour casts being imposed by the variable colour temperature of artificial light, and will also help to ensure the card is evenly lit.

If you decide to record your titles using the camera adopted for the wedding pictures, you will almost certainly have to employ the MACRO setting of the lens.

In this mode the lens has little *depth of field* and so great care must be taken to ensure that the plane of the caption card and the camera are precisely parallel.

One of the best ways of doing this is to look at the view of the camera through a TV set rather than the camera's monitor. The larger screen will immediately show up any poor focusing due to the card not being correctly placed.
Since the actual recording of the titles is a very real part of the post-production process, the precise way of doing this will be deferred to the next chapter which is more concerned with the artistic refinement of the film, rather than the technology being covered here.

8
Adding the Professional Touch

Special Occasion Video Guide

The first task that should be undertaken before working on your carefully-recorded tapes, is to make a note of every shot on each tape, together with details of exactly where it can be located.

This sounds a boring job, but in fact will make editing very much simpler in the long run. Indeed, this special replaying of the tapes will give the opportunity to form ideas on the best way to arrange the sequence of shots to get the best results.

It is important that you use the same equipment intended for editing for the very simple reason than tape counters vary from one machine to the next, and accurate location of the start and end of each shot will save much time later.

Professional VCRs are able to number each individual *frame* of the tape, thus giving tremendous accuracy when locating an edit point. Domestic VCRs use a different method, and derive the tape counter numbers by timing the passage of the tape past a particular point in the machine.

Observation of the linear speed of tape travel will show how difficult it is to build an accurate tape counter. Indeed, the number of frames that may pass over a one-digit change on the counter, could be as many as twenty-five to thirty!

This should give you an idea of why making artistically perfect edits is an extremely difficult task. Several attempts may be necessary and even then the result may be far from the achievements of the professional!

The drawing on the opposite page suggests a connection arrangement for a basic editing system. It does not make use of advanced equipment such as the titling camera and editing console –this is shown later.

Even so, the simple arrangement illustrated will permit the addition of title captions or perhaps scenes from still photographs, as well as the all-important addition of sound from alternative sources.

Stereo-to-mono connection leads are available from most good retail outlets and may be needed because the output of most audio recorders is stereo, whereas most camcorders record in mono. Here, the two

Adding the Professional Touch

tracks of the stereo recording are added together, giving a single output for connection to the master VCR.

In extremis, a suitable adaptor lead can be made up by a qualified service engineer, or where the reader feels the job is easy enough to tackle, the parts are readily obtained from a good hi-fi or electronic components shop.

Set up the equipment on a convenient table - it may mean dismantling part of your home hi-fi and TV systems to do this but it is vital to have everything within easy reach.

For convenience, we will call the final full version of the recording the *master* tape, because it will become the 'parent' from which offspring duplicates are made for distribution to relatives and friends.
The material recorded at the time of the wedding will be called the *'original'* tape.

When checking through the tapes to write the editing notes, include the tapes you used to record the incidental and 'atmosphere' scenes as well as those recorded at the wedding itself.

A useful form can be drawn up to act as a reminder of the details needed during editing.

After carefully zeroing the counter with the tape transport set in the PAUSE PLAY mode, start the tape running. Play the tape and, as it runs through, note the following points.

1. The counter number at the start of the scene.

2. How did the shot open? Was it with a simple CUT, a FADE-IN, a change from unfocused to FOCUSed view, a ZOOM back or forwards, or a rapid SWEEP PAN. If it was the last, in which direction was the camera panning, left to right, or right to left?

3. Make a brief note of the content of the scene.

4. How did the shot close? Was it a CUT, ZOOM, SWEEP PAN, deFOCUS or a FADE and if the fade was to a coloured blank screen, what was the colour?

5. Were there any defects in the shot which should be removed?

6. Was the sound-track OK?

Special Occasion Video Guide

7. The counter number at the end of the scene.

The next few pages illustrate **the process with examples** taken from an entirely fictional wedding film and incidental shots. The notes will also form the basis of the illustrations which demonstrate how the post-production processes work.

This series of shots, on two separate tapes, is far from the complete sequence that will have been recorded on the wedding day. However, it will serve to show how continuity can be added to make a complete story unfold. For a start, the existing sequence is missing at least one important element of the finished production - the titles. This is where you can now go on to work out the correct sequence for the shots already recorded, and produce notes for those still needed. Use a form similar to that already used for the existing production notes, leaving space between each entry to indicate how the shots are to be linked.

Tape 1. Mostly incidental, atmosphere and test shots taken prior to the wedding day.

0000. Cut into medium long shot of church path and entrance. Pans to the right to view the road containing traffic similar to the wedding day. Cut end. Sound track has unwanted voices on. Shot OK.

0012. Cut into steeply angled shot of bell tower, panning slowly down to open church door. Sound - quiet traffic noise from behind camera. Shot OK.

0019. Sweep pan to left showing path of church from church door. Arrival of groom for rehearsal (No good for final film). Groom walks towards camera. **Do not use!**

0030- 0151. Rehearsal scenes - **Do not use!**

0151. Cut into long shot of stained glass window. Held steady. Shot OK. Sound track has nothing of use. Cut end.

0159. Fade into close up of flowers, zoom back to show pulpit and

Adding the Professional Touch

front row of pews. Sound track is organ practicing - no use! Shot OK.

0169. Cut to medium shot of organ pipes, panning down to show church organist. Sound track no use, but shot OK. Cut end

0180. End of recordings.

Tape 2. Recordings taken of the ceremony on the wedding day.

0000. Cut to wide angle view of guests outside church, pan right to more guests standing at church gate. Sound track OK. Cut end.

0019. Cut to arrival of groom by car, pan left showing him moving from car to guests and then going into church. Cut end. Sound OK.

0031. Cut to close -up of vicar in porch, slowly zooming back to reveal him talking to bridesmaids, slow pan right to show empty church path. Sound track start is a bit awkward but generally OK. Cut end.

0037. Long shot from RH side of church gate showing bride's car in distance. Sound OK. Cut end.,

0040. Cut to closer view of bride's car, zoom back to keep back door of car in shot. car stops, bride gets out with father, greeted by vicar, Pan left to follow her walking up path. Cut end.

0061. Inside church - cut into waist length shot of bride and father adjusting their dress for walk up aisle. Shot held and panned right to follow them up aisle - camera left running - end of sequence a mess, but sound OK.

0083. Side view of bride and groom at choir steps, faced by vicar. Vicar asks for objections. Pan right to show guests and cuts when no answer received! Sound OK. Cut end.

0092. Cut to side view of bride and groom making vows, shot ends with pan to close up of ring exchange. Cut end.

Special Occasion Video Guide

0105. Sweep pan to right - ends by showing back of guests in church singing hymn and bride and groom at choir steps with vicar. Cut end.

0120. Cut into long shot of bride and groom walking to registry, followed by parents.

Note: The correct tape is indicated by its number, followed by an oblique stroke separating it from the counter number showing on the replay machine at the start of the shot. The counter number at the end of the scene is shown separately.

1. Fade from green blank screen to title card. Hold for approx 30 secs, or some useful break in the introductory music. Fade out to green screen.
2. Cut to Tape 1/ 0000 - cut at 0012. Continue title music throughout- check timing for a suitable break before or during next scene.
3. Cut to Tape 2/0000 - cut at 0031 using next shot as well.
4. Cut to Tape 1/0159 - replace sound track with wild sound - cut at 0169.
5. Cut to Tape 2/0031 (check sound start and go to counter 0032 is possible). Fade in wild sound track at about 0060 and continue through next shot until cut is indicated. Cut at 0072 or earlier if poor technique obtrudes. Check wild sound track to ensure wedding march finishes at the end of the shot - cut wild sound.
6. Cut to Tape 2/0083. End this section by going straight through two shots. Cut at 0120. Start wild sound track from 0105.
7. Cut to Tape 1/0151 using continuation of wild sound track through from previous shot. Cut at 0159. Continue wild sound track to...
8. Cut to Tape 2/ 0120. End shot at cut end 0135.

Adding the Professional Touch

Finding a suitable ending for your film can be difficult. Here is one simple but effective idea: letter a still picture of the couple with appropriate words, cover it with a clear, self-sealing film, then film a sequence of confetti being lightly blown across the photograph.

The table on page 114 shows how our mythical wedding video recording is to be edited into a continuous whole. References to sound-track editing appear a little later in this chapter.

Titles add to continuity

A look at the titling techniques used by professionals will quickly reveal a whole bag of tricks, most of which are unfortunately not feasible for an amateur to adopt when using the type of equipment normally available.

Briefly, titles for older films were usually displayed as a simple series of text frames with or without drawn illustrations. Often, the transition between one title sequence and the next would have been a simple cut.

Later films developed the technique of dissolving from one title to the next. A simple and popular method was to scroll the complete text past the camera, usually from the bottom to the top of the screen.

As film technology progressed, text titles were *overlayed* on top of still or sometimes moving scenes drawn from the film itself. However, it was still necessary to either dissolve or scroll from one screen full of text, to the next.

Much work was done to make titles more interesting. Quite a big step occurred with the introduction of cartoon animation since it then became possible to animate text - or even to overlay text on animated figures.

This development occurred at the same time new optical techniques were evolved making a host of other tricks possible.

Although many of these ideas cannot easily be applied by the amateur, it is surprising how the use of a little ingenuity will produce more-than-satisfactory results.

For example, using the facilities available on the portable or camcorder, you can consider commencing the final production, recording a coloured blank screen which then fades into a title. This could be made from transfer lettering placed on a clear film which then overlays a still

Adding the Professional Touch

photograph relevant to the film content.

If you have a 'tame' artist, an effective alternative is to have the title card painted - ideally in pastel shades as these are rendered more accurately than primary colours.

Where a preprinted card, such as the blank wedding invitation, has been selected for use, difficulties could be encountered since such cards are often printed on white using a silver printing ink. This does not reproduce very well on a TV screen!

There could also be a lesser problem - that the card is the wrong shape to fit the screen format.

The first of these two difficulties may be overcome by borrowing a bit of still-camera equipment. Many keen photographers have a selection of coloured filters to put over the lens to give special effects. By using one of these, held over the video camera

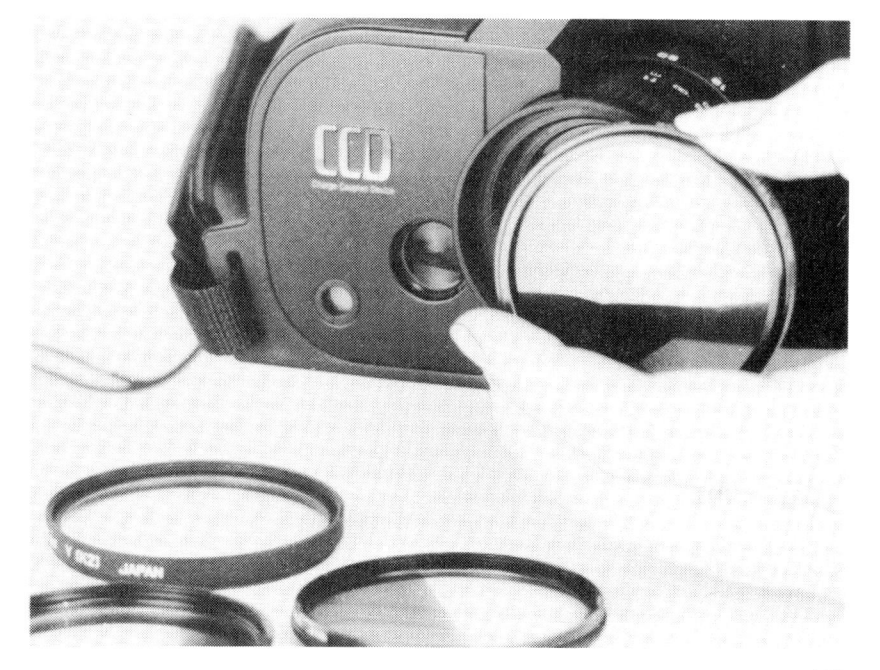

Video camera lenses usually have the same kind of screw thread encircling the front glass as do still camera lenses. Therefore, given a matching diameter, the wide range of photographic filters can be utilised to add, say, a light pastel tint to an otherwise fairly bland, straightforward shot such as the wedding invitation.

119

Special Occasion Video Guide

A colourful way of using the wedding invitation as part of the introductory sequence to your film.

lens, the colours of the card may be sufficiently altered to make them more legible.

In the second instance, where the shape of the original does not fit the TV frame, try laying the card on a sheet of similar paper or perhaps on a table top with some trinkets or just a vase of flowers.

By starting the sequence showing a broad view of the table, and then homing in on the card using zoom, the title sequence can be given some animation to capture the viewer's imagination. A good sound-track will also help to add some artistic emphasis to the technique.

This type of consideration points up the fact that the purpose of the title sequence is to let your audience know what the film is about and something about the principal participants. It should also set a mood, allowing the viewers the chance to develop a feeling of anticipation.

It is one of the most important parts of the video recording left to be done, and gives the film-maker an opportunity for artistic expression. The correct combination of aural and visual effect can considerably add to the professional appearance of your production.

The question of how long a title sequence should be held on screen is very difficult to answer exactly. Often it may be determined by the sound sequence selected to accompany the image. Deciding the right timing is again going to be a matter of experiment.

At the very least, the title sequence should be on screen long enough for the slowest reader to take in the entire text, but should never be held so long that the viewer starts getting bored waiting for something else to happen!

This is not so true of the end caption which, ideally, should be recorded in the same session as the title caption. In this case, a good sound-track may justify a quite lengthy sequence.

Adding the Professional Touch

The point here is that the selection of the sounds to be used with title and end captions is worth some thought. It is not just a question of the appropriate style of music or sound - it is also a question of whether it is the right length.

Bearing in mind that continuity may be added to a series of scenes by running the sound-track through scene transitions. It may be worthwhile following the title sequence with one of the 'atmosphere' shots recorded prior to the wedding.

In the example given in the editing notes on page 114, this is precisely the method I have adopted, first to give a sense of continuity and second to take advantage of an existing atmosphere shot to set the scene.

Another feature of the example is to start with a blank coloured screen and fade into the titles, finally fading out to another blank screen for a brief period.

There are two reasons for doing this. First, most VCRs take a short time to synchronise the picture at the very start of the

Special Occasion Video Guide

tape. This shows up as a brief burst of white lines travelling across the screen.

To avoid this intruding on the impact you wish to make with the opening titles, start with a blank screen. Of course, it will look absolutely intentional if the screen is coloured, and this can be generated by the camcorder or camera if it incorporates the right features.

The second reason for using this idea is because it provides a very gentle and smooth transition which draws the viewer on and into the main part of the recording itself.

So far I have given very little idea of how the titles can be technically incorporated into the master copy of the final production. This is where it may be an advantage if the camcorder or portable which is being used to replay the original raw material takes a full sized tape.

If this is so, then the title sequence, minus its sound-track, can be recorded by the camera directly on to the master tape. It has the advantage of eliminating an extra process of editing and dubbing, while ensuring that picture quality remains as high as possible.

In the event that you only have a C-format camera, then this will have to be used to record the titles, and the results subsequently copied to the master tape.

On several occasions, mention has been made of the use of sound from sources other than the original sound-track. Since the editing of the sound-track is a topic by itself, a separate section is devoted to it. Suffice to say that in dealing with the editing of the picture elements, sound will normally be transferred as well, even though it may be erased and a new sound source substituted afterwards.

The third edit of our example is where careful use of the camcorder during the recording of the wedding has made it possible to use two successive shots apparently without any work being done during the transfer from original to master.

Regrettably, this is not always the case. If, for example, the camera user accidentally advanced the blank tape after reviewing the most recent shot, and then proceeded to record

Adding the Professional Touch

the next scene, leaving a small gap of blank tape between the two shots, then problems could arise during editing.

This is really a repetition of the sort of situation described earlier, when a tape is first started in a VCR. The speed at which the tape runs through the machine, and the relationship of the video head drum to the tape is determined by the presence of special control signals recorded on the tape. These provide synchronising marks to ensure that the image is scanned correctly.

If, for some reason, the video head drum gets out of correct synchronism, white *noise bars* will appear on the screen and move either up or down until synchronism is regained, at which point they disappear.

Video camcorders get stopped and started many times between the beginning and the end of a tape. Nevertheless, synchronism is automatically maintained from one shot to the next, because the camera either stops and locks the tape in place, or the camera electronics scan the last section of recorded tape to pick up the synchronising marks and position the tape correctly for the next shot.

The camera cannot do this, not because it has been switched to wind, rewind, or replay modes, and assumes that it should carry on from the end of the last recorded section.

If a mistake is made, and a tape is wound between shots, then the only way of recovering the situation is to replay the existing recording to a point very near the end of the last shot and then, if the camera has *back-space edit* facilities, record the next scene using this feature.

Where back-space edit is not available and the user wants to avoid difficulties during editing, an attempt should be made to start the subsequent shot on top of the last few seconds of the previous recording.

This may produce a slight 'jump' in the picture, but is really the only answer to the problem.

This underlines a principle of editing when using simple equipment. Because the VCR containing the master tape has to be stopped and started many times, the editing operator is recommended to hold the machine in PAUSE while locating the next original shot to be transferred. In this way, synchronism will be maintained throughout the master and noise bars will be avoided.

If you are transferring from a tape suffering from faulty synchronism, PAUSE the master during the affected section, restarting it when the picture from the original has re-stabilised.

Wild versus synchronised sound

During the detailed checking of the original tapes, notes were made of points where, although picture content was fine, the sound-track was occasionally poor or unsuitable.

However, in the previous section of this chapter there have been several examples of using an alternative sound source as a substitute for the original.

There is yet a third option. This is where the sound-track on the original tape might be very useful, but the picture is of no value; or where the sound recorded is not directly linked to the picture.

If the sound is recorded and the source of the sound is pictured in such a way that one can link the sound to the picture, then it is logical that the two go together.

But what if you have recorded, say, the backs of the church congregation singing a hymn. The chances are that you could de-synchronise the picture and sound without anyone being the wiser!

The relevance of this might be more obvious if we take a closer look at the way the sound-track of the master has been scheduled in the editing notes.

The titles appear on the screen, accompanied perhaps by the sound of church bells, or organ music, both of which might have been recorded with a wild-sound machine, or even using an extract from a record.

It is entirely possible that the sound section to be used is too long for the timing of the title shot: in our example, it has been suggested that the sound will continue into the shot following the second edit (i.e. after Tape 1/0000, but before 0012.)

Adding the Professional Touch

But then we are left with the background traffic noise recorded the day before the wedding - as was the picture. Really, what would be better is to have sounds which give a better feeling of the day itself.

Now this might be found on Tape 2 from 0000 to 0019 - the scene of the guests talking among each other while waiting for the bride. Perhaps this sound could be 'lifted' by recording a duplicate audio tape from the original video tape. This can then be used to dub back to the master at any point.

In this particular example, the solution is not ideal, because the pictures shot take longer than the sound-track, so the two do not end together. However, this begins to emphasize the value of leaving the camera to run without necessarily recording any important visual events, but simply to gain a bit of extra wild sound-track which might

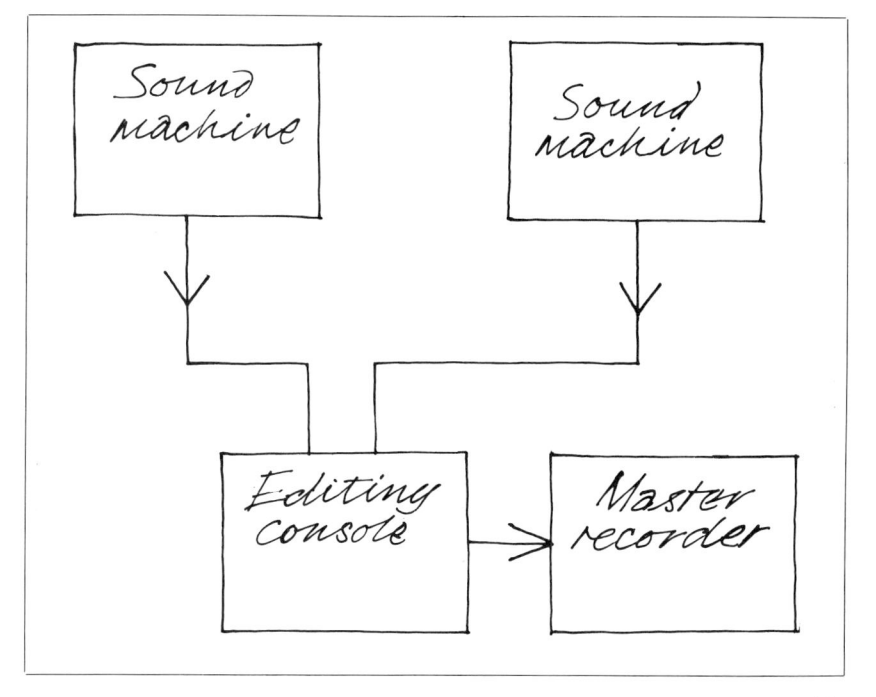

The connection arrangements for a typical and simple editing system incorporating a wild sound recorder.

be used later.

Another rather complex possibility available to the advanced enthusiast, is illustrated in the diagram on the opposite page. Here, two sound machines are feeding into an editing console where the sounds are mixed and balanced, and then passed on to the master recorder.

This would make it possible, for example, to mix the sound of bells with the recorded snatches of conversation that might have been lifted from an otherwise useless shot.

Edit 5 in our example is a case where synchronism of sound and image is of no importance, and the available recording from the wild-sound machine has been used very effectively to provide continuity between one shot and the next.

All these techniques are made possible because the master recorder offers an audio-dubbing facility.

This is not to say that alternative sound-tracks cannot be added during the post-production stages, but a new and very real difficulty then emerges which might prove too much to overcome.

The diagram on page 125 illustrates a possible way of editing the sound-track when audio-dub is not available on the master.

The extra equipment required is a suitable hi-fi amplifier which has tape input sockets of the phono variety - in other words, there is one plug for the left channel and another for the right. The audio signal from the video playback machine is fed to one of the sockets.

The other socket is used for a feed from the wild-sound recorder, but because most audio tape machines record a stereo signal, an adaptor lead will be needed to convert its sound to mono.

A second stereo to mono adaptor lead will be needed at the TAPE OUT sockets of the amplifier, to provide a connection to the mono audio input of the master VCR.

Now, if there are enough hands available (and this may be where the problems start!) and a great sense of unanimity of timing, it may prove possible, using the balance control of the

Adding the Professional Touch

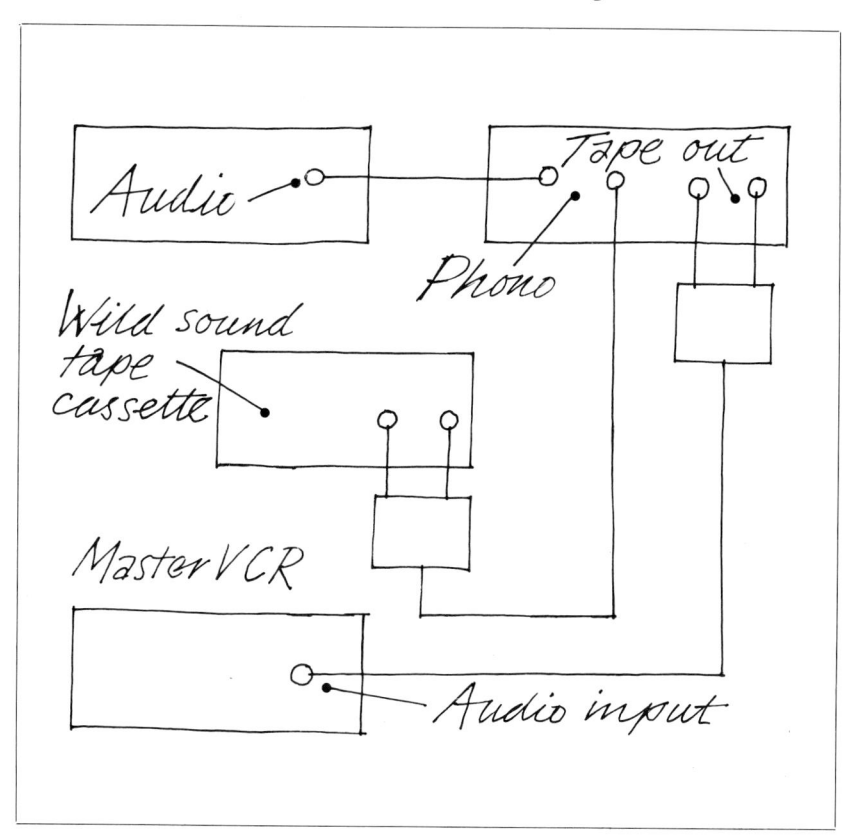

stereo amplifier, to mix or substitute the sound-track of the original during the actual process of transferring the image! However, first practise this on some spare tape.

The complexity of the technical arrangements, coupled to the requirement for three or four hands all working in total unison make this kind of editing arrangement an enormous challenge. A lot of practice and patience will be needed before the end result is anywhere near perfect.

In the long run, it will pay to seek out a master VCR that offers audio-dubbing facilities!

Here, two sound machines are feeding into an editing console where the sounds are mixed and balanced, and then passed on to the master recorder.

Throwing the confetti as bride and groom leave the church or registry office — authorities permitting — will provide you will a colourful and happy sequence, shots which could prove useful, say, at the end of the film as well as in their proper chronological sequence.

Do be certain that you will have sufficient lighting at the reception to be able to film informal scenes such as this. However, it is equally important that the lighting should not be over-bright, dazzling your subjects and forcing them to avoid your lens.

These shots illustrate the problems of a buffet reception, where you have to be quick enough to film the 'spread' before it vanishes, and also be able to follow bride and groom to their seats to ensure a clear shot before their guests join them. (Naturally, you should not expect to eat yourself!) Again, your tactful 'minder' can help here, restraining people for the few minutes you require. If you can persuade one of the catering staff to perform this role, so much the better.

9
The Oops! Factor

Special Occasion Video Guide

Making a home video may start by looking rather easy, indeed, if the project is regarded as nothing more than an electronic version of the familiar home movies then your impression is probably correct.

However, in this age of sophisticated television, the large number of features available in a domestic video camera has led to the creation of a whole new hobby. This is video film making - something which can closely emulate the professional efforts seen on television.

Perhaps this book has given the reader some idea of the wide gap that exists between the older technology of the home movie, and the new possibilities that can be applied in any serious attempt at a family documentary.

New concepts and skills have been evolved which at first look a bit mind-boggling, but in fact require nothing more than the use of common sense logic:

The Oops! Factor

the harder task is realising their potential to the full.

At this stage, if you have tried some of the things described in this book, it will come as no surprise to discover that mistakes can be made - even by the professionals! It is simply a natural part of the learning process and nine times out of ten there will be a way to recover the situation.

This is no consolation for an irrecoverable shot but there are even ways out of that disaster! Sometimes it can be done in such a way that viewers of the final production have no idea what has happened and conclude that you are simply applying a bit of artistic licence to the production.

The purpose of this chapter is obvious from its title - it deals with the sort of clangers you may have made and tries to offer some solutions which cover up or rectify the mistake.

Of course, there are some things which cannot be solved - the most ridiculous of which is forgetting to take any video tape with you on the day. Fortunately there are few people as absent-minded as that!

There was no plan!

Perhaps the most basic mistake is to think that you can make a video film of a wedding, or a baptism, a sports event or a family party without going through a process of careful planning.

I am sure that some readers will consider the whole business of making a storyboard, checking the layout of the locations and making provision for difficult sound recording problems, a real chore!

Special Occasion Video Guide

Every one will try to dispense with planning from time to time but the question will remain, 'How can the task be accomplished without ending up with a rag-bag of shots that will rapidly bore you and your viewers?'

A salutary starting point is to remember the interminable holiday slide show that some relatives put us through every year. The problem is not one of sharing a photographic experience with them, but that there are just too many pictures - and many of them of no interest to you or anyone else outside their family group.

If only they would make a careful selection and cut out all the pictures which record something of personal interest to them alone!

That should give you a clue, start recording as much as possible to give plenty of material to make a selection from, and then reduce it by tough editing to get to the core of material of interest to the largest audience.

In recording as much as possible, also try to leave the camera running with the microphone pointing in favourable directions, even when there is little of interest going on visually.

The extra sound-track will be very valuable when it comes to providing continuity by running sound-track through scene changes at the editing stage.

However, the fact that you failed to make good plans and a storyboard before the wedding, does not render the planning needed for good post-production unnecessary.

Indeed, it will be even more to ensure that you make the best of what will become a difficult job.

132

Batteries not charged?

This is a favourite mistake since no battery ever shows its state of charge simply by looking at it. The first indication of failure you will probably get is that either the recorder will fail to work, or a warning will appear in the viewfinder at - usually the worst possible moment!

Dependent on when the problem shows itself, there are few ways out of this difficulty. If there is still time before the wedding, just try recharging for as long as possible. Some batteries having a small capacity take a surprisingly short time to recharge.

If there is little or no time, see if there is a way of running the machine from the mains. In the case of many C-format cameras and all portable recorders with separate cameras, the machine can be run from the charger unit which itself plugs into a mains socket.

For example, camcorders have separate battery chargers, some of which have a socket and lead making it possible to connect and run the camcorder from the mains. (So remember to take along an extension cable with a mains plug!)

This is extremely useful when editing, since this takes time and consumes a lot of power. It is not so handy when recording on the spot because the length of the battery charger lead may be a restriction -especially when filming outside.

In the case of portable recorders, utilising the battery recharger can be more difficult, because it may form part of the tuner unit.

The combined problem of having to deal with the camera, a portable recorder joined to the tuner by a short lead or through a direct link obtained when clipping the units together, and a mains lead as well is really very difficult!

Frankly, forgetting to fully charge the batteries before going out to record the wedding is one disaster you really should have avoided!

Forget to plug the mic in?

You will know by now that some cameras and camcorders have microphones that can be exchanged for a different type.

Just suppose you did a swop at some time, and then removed the accessory microphone, forgetting to plug the regular version back in.

The result of doing this is not too much of a disaster. The camera will still record the pictures but will have a totally silent sound-track.

This is where the advantages of having a wild sound-track may save the day. However, one thing you will not be able to do is to synchronise the sounds with the events on the screen.

Typically, you may have made a wild sound-track of the vicar, bride and groom going through the wedding vows. The lips of any of these might be seen moving, but getting the wild sound-track to synchronise with them will prove well nigh impossible!

In this case, do not even try it - just sort out which of the two recordings will be the most important to the viewers, the sound, or the pictures. If it is the former, then the sound-track may be used to back a spare shot of the church architecture perhaps recorded during a rehearsal.

You might even have recorded the street outside the church during a trial visit. You could use this, backed by the sound-track of the vows being exchanged. The idea might sound strange, but could be accepted by the viewer as a piece of artistic licence.

Providing that the editing is done with care, you might be able to make use of parts of the silent picture recording, backed by sounds which come 'off camera'.

Consider this idea. Perhaps in the offending scenes, the vicar had his back to the camera and the only face you could see fully was the groom's. This makes it possible to intercut incidental atmosphere shots

The Oops! Factor

during the groom's responses, but return to the shot of the couple for everything else.

In such a case, the lack of synchronism with the wild sound-track becomes of no importance.

The real difficulty that might arise is when there is no wild sound recording to substitute for the missing sound-track.

In this case, you will have to resort to dubbing suitable music or sounds which obviously originate from somewhere else.

Here are a few ideas worth trying. Make a tape recording of the sounds in a children's playground. If the children are playing games involving laughter, or perhaps singing, such a sound-track accompanying the pictures of the couple exchanging vows might suggest a romance which stretches back to childhood, or perhaps the promise of children to come! Be careful though - there can be a danger in being too farsighted.

Another thought is to use a 'joke' musical item. Something like 'Get Me to the Church on Time', from 'My Fair Lady' (duly noting copyright requirements).

There are several other pieces of music which might usefully be slotted into this gap.

A similar technique can be used to replace missing sound-track from other parts of the occasion.

However, the biggest problem will always be where the picture tells the viewer, that they should be hearing some particular sound. Normally this is indicated by lip movements. In rare circumstances, you may be forced to cut the offending scene completely out of the final production.

There is not enough light!

This really is a tough one, because the whole purpose of making a wedding video is to have pictures.

Hopefully the shortage of light will affect only a small part of the total event. Just how you deal with the situation depends on the importance of the action taking place at that particular moment - and the reasons for the poor illumination.

135

Special Occasion Video Guide

First, a video camera will continue to record something, even if the viewfinder monitor screen is showing a warning that the light levels are too low. Just how much will be seen on the screen - and how it will look - can only be found out by experiment.

Try recording a few seconds and then press the REVIEW button to replay the recording through the viewfinder. This will at least give an idea if any image is being recorded - though it will not tell you the quality of the colour rendition.

Bear in mind that when the light levels are too low, the first evidence of the fact that will be seen on the TV screen will be in the form of *chroma noise*.

This distortion of the colours and the spotty appearance of the picture may not be too bad a problem - providing that the scenes concerned are only a small part of the whole recording.

Using existing artificial lights may be some sort of a solution. For example, you may well find that the church is darker than expected, the vicar having not arranged for the lights to be turned on.

Try switching on any such lighting since, though it may be far from adequate, it will improve the situation, turning things away from what may have been a disaster.

Fortunately, the artificial lighting in the reception rooms should be good enough to get reasonable pictures in an emergency.

However, there is always the possibility that the room lights could fail. Perhaps a fuse has blown, or worse, the supply has been cut off!

In this case, candles may be the only solution. Some camcorders and cameras are sensitive enough so that they will even record a picture in candlelight.

Running out of tape?

Although there is little point in saying this should not happen, you obviously need a way to get round the crisis.

There are two possible solutions - first, get someone to go and get you more tape while you eke out the remainder of your supply.

The second possibility is dependent upon the video system you are using. Some offer the possibility of recording at Long Play speeds. This will double the recording time left available to you, which may save the day.

It is possible to record both LP and SP scenes on the same tape, though, on replay, there may be a moment or two as the replay VCR adjusts to the lower tape speeds. For this reason, you should start the LP recording a second or two before taping anything of importance, giving some space to cut the speed change interference from the edited version of the tape.

Picture quality, and more particularly the sound quality, will suffer when compared to the SP recordings, but you will be able to continue recording when otherwise you may have been forced to stop short.

Forget the tripod?

From the practice recording made before the wedding day itself, you will have learned that it is extremely difficult to get steady pictures when the zoom lens is at full telephoto extension.

This is where a heavy camera designed for use on the shoulder is an advantage, since the extra support provides the needed stability.

Smaller cameras, which are

Special Occasion Video Guide

just hand held, are more problematic. The small size, coupled to light weight make them more difficult to hold steadily. This rarely shows up when the lens is adjusted in wide angle, or a mid-focal length but can be all-too apparent in telephoto mode.

Getting around the lack of a tripod needs a bit of ingenuity. Try holding the camera against a solid object, such as a pillar, a tree trunk or a gate post.

In extremis, use the shoulder of a friend. By standing behind someone, and resting the camera on their shoulder, you may gain enough stability to avoid camera shake.

There is another advantage; your friend is probably more easily moved around than a tripod!

People getting in the way?

All but the tallest camera users have a problem. People can often be in the way, just when you need that vital shot.

Of course, you could always ask them to move, but this is not always an easy thing to do - especially as any such comments or requests may be recorded on the sound-track.

For a few scenes, a handy lightweight stepladder may provide the answer. It will mean you also need a willing assistant to set it up or move it.

More importantly, using a stepladder will severely limit the way in which you can use the camera. A tracking shot, where the camera is moved from one place to another, is just not possible on a ladder - unless you have made the most elaborate arrangements to put the ladder on a mobile platform!

The Oops! Factor

Two other possibilities exist - find a high spot from which you can see the action - or employ a professional photographers' trick.

By setting the zoom lens to a wide angle and holding the camera at arm's length over your head, you may obtain an uninterrupted view. The fact that you cannot see through the viewfinder and thus your camera may not be pointing in exactly the right direction may not matter too much.

Since a wide angle setting has been used, the camera can be pointing slightly off the correct direction but still include the parts of the scene you wish to record.

As a last resort, just start the camera recording then hand it to someone taller, or nearer the front of the crowd.

Not allowed to record the ceremony?

This is a problem that quite frequently arises. It may be the wedding is being held in a registry office and the registrar bans all use of cameras.

Alternatively, the vicar, priest, rabbi or whoever is conducting the ceremony considers that cameras are an unwanted intrusion.

Normally, you will have discovered this during the early planning stages. Getting over the problem without causing offence, and at the same time making the recording feel complete will call on your finest creative abilities.

Some of the ideas I offer here may not be possible, but will perhaps give you a basis for coming up with workable alternatives.

For example, where you may not be able to use a camera, recording the sound alone with a discreet wild-sound recorder and microphone could get you part of the way.

Special Occasion Video Guide

Once you have a sound-track, you only need to provide appropriate pictures that will blend into the mood of the moment. This will certainly involve you in much preparatory recording.

Try getting the couple out together for a day, wandering around the shops or in the local park for example. Get as much on tape as possible and then carefully edit the results to produce a sequence which complements the sound-track.

Where this may not be possible, because the bride or groom are unavailable when you need them, ask to see their photograph albums and select some still pictures that might be intercut with 'atmosphere' recordings made before the wedding or even on the day itself.

Record scenes of the building being used for the ceremony, attractive shrubs and blooms, or perhaps the last-minute preparations going on at the reception.
All these things can be carefully cut to produce a visual backing to the sound-track.

Later in the day, record a close up of the rings being exchanged and the groom kissing the bride, then cut these into place at the appropriate moments in the sound-track. However, make sure that you do not include anything in the picture that gives away the fact that the shot was recorded at a different time.

Devices like this are no substitute for a complete recording of the actual ceremony, but if you have planned a way around the difficulty, the final and edited recording will appear as complete as possible given the circumstances.

Editing problems

Editing the component parts of the recording to make a smooth and continuous production may give rise to a number of unforeseen difficulties.

Some of these may happen just through inexperience; other because of genuine technical problems. Usually, it will be obvious where the problem lies.

In the notes which follow, remember that the 'master' tape and recorder is the machine and tape on which you are compiling the edited version of the tape.

The 'original' tapes are those used in the camera system on the wedding day, or during the preparation of titles.

One of the most difficult tasks will be to time the cuts from one scene to another when the scenes in question are at two different points on the original tape, or when two originals are being used.

In the majority of cases, the 'join' between two scenes that have been edited together may be obvious because of a momentary spasm of interference that appears on the screen when replaying the final result.

This usually occurs because there is a fault in the synchronism between one shot and the next. Normally, this would be avoided if the master machine is used properly when making the edit.

Never press the STOP button if you have not finished the editing process - use the PAUSE control. This ensures that the timing pulses which the VCR uses to time the start of each scan of the TV screen are recorded in the correct position on the tape.

When the stop button is used, the tape unlaces itself from the tape transport and is returned to the cassette. When the RECORD/PAUSE buttons are pressed, the tape has to be withdrawn from the cassette, laced back around the transport system and repositioned to start the next scene at the end of the previous recording.

Sometimes this involved process results in some slight errors in the position of the tape. The next scene recorded is thus marginally out of place, and the TV set has to take a fraction of a second sorting out the timing error and re-synchronising itself.

All this can be avoided by using the PAUSE button, because in this case, the tape is left threaded in the transport and held locked until restarted.

However, there may be some occasions when it is undesirable to leave the master machine in PAUSE. It could be that it is going to take a long time to prepare the next original to be transferred. In this case there is no choice but to stop the

Special Occasion Video Guide

master.

This is where the INSERT control on the master machine will prove invaluable. When you are ready to recommence the editing session, play back the last few seconds of the edited tape, PAUSING the machine just a second or two before the end of the previous scene.

Now, holding the insert button, press PAUSE once again. At this point, you will be ready to slot in the next scene. However, to start the master machine, you will have to press the PLAY button - *not* RECORD!

At the end of recording the new sequence, return to the PAUSE mode as in the normal situation.

Note: The above method of using the INSERT control applies only to certain makes of VCR. Check the manual for your machine to make sure there are no variations before you attempt to record.

The wrong scene?

After completing the editing process, you may find that a mistake has been made, and a wrong shot has been used.

Providing that there are no big differences in the length of the unwanted and the wanted shots, it is possible to replace one by the other using the INSERT editing control.

Once again, the problem is to ensure that the beginning and end points of the newly inserted section are not marred by obvious jumps or inteference on the TV screen.

The INSERT facility does this by making sure that the timing of starting frame of the picture matches the existing shots.

The problem is ensuring that the new scene ends at the right point and you avoid the danger of erasing something important that might follow.

Start by checking through the scene you do not want, pressing the PAUSE button at the precise point you wish to end the insert. At that point, RESET the tape counter and press the MEMORY button.

Doing this ensures that the recorder will remember where to stop the INSERT. Now REWIND to the point where you wish to start the insert, using the picture search mode of the VCR. Press PAUSE.

Now you are ready to place the new shot in between existing scenes. Your original tape should have been wound to a point just before the beginning of the shot you wish to insert. This is important because you then have time to start the original and get back to the master machine to press the PLAY button to start the insert.

On some odd occasions, you may have made a mistake and want to stop the insert before you reach the edit point marked by the MEMORY.

The best way to do this is to avoid pressing STOP - which just causes picture jumps, but instead, press the tape counter RESET button. This will make the master machine switch to playback, after which it can be stopped or paused.

Camera stopped unexpectedly?

Those of you who have scanned through the previous section, may realise that the tape counter has some importance to the other operating function of the camcorder or portable VCR.

In fact, on all machines it not only registers the length of tape passed through the transport since the RESET point, it may also mark an arbitrary point where you may wish to return at a later time.

The demanding part is remembering exactly what it is doing - and cancelling any unwanted function that may have been programmed through the MEMORY button.

Ideally, you should always rewind a tape back to the beginning , RESET the counter to zero and check that the MEMORY, if there is one, is switched off until needed.

However, you may load a tape which has been partially used, and want to avoid having to go back to the beginning and then finding the end of the previous recording once again.

This is fine - and there is no problem, providing you remember what you have done, since the tape counter now does not know about the used part of the tape, and assumes it is at the beginning. It simply counts from the point you loaded the tape.

This also means it will probably stop at that point when you next operate the REWIND button. To get past that point and back to the

Special Occasion Video Guide

beginning of the tape, you will have to press REWIND a second time!

The simple rule of thumb is to always check the memory and the tape counter if the machine stops unexpectedly. The problem is almost certainly located there.

My TV howls when I try to record titles!

In fact, your TV might howl at any time when it is being used to monitor the pictures being recorded via a camera.

This is a problem well known to studio sound engineers and occurs when the microphone starts picking up sounds from the loudspeaker of the TV set, and then promptly feeds them back via the recorder to the TV set again.

The end result is a whistling or howling noise which obliterates any sounds you really intended to pick up.

Of course, if you are recording titles, no sound will be needed anyway since you will probably be dubbing a sound-track from another source. In this case, unplug the microphone!

A simple solution in other cases, where you need the microphone to be in action, is to turn the TV sound down to a minimum. If you need to check the quality of the sound during recording, use headphones!

The replayed pictures look awful!

There might be any number of reasons for this and you need to analyse the way in which the picture has been affected to decide the reasons.

For example, you may recall that coloured spots which affect reds in particular are an indication of chroma noise. If the effect is present in the original, this is usually a reliable indication there was not enough light illuminating the scene you were recording.

But suppose you see this appear on the master, or on one of your duplicates of the master, yet it is not noticeable on the original.

If it appears on the master, then the problem will usually be that the original recording is marginal - the light levels were only just enough - or the tape you have used for the master is of insufficient quality.

It is vital you use the best tape possible for the master in order to preserve as much of the original as possible.

Every stage of transfer from one tape to another will result in a slight loss of picture quality. This will be most noticeable in colour rendition. If you make too many transfers, no matter how good the tapes you have used, faults will begin to appear - **do not blame the tape in this case.**

But suppose you begin to get lines of white spots (called snow) dancing across the screen. Usually this is not an indication that the tape is scratched or faulty. More often than not the problem will be that you have accidentally shifted the TRACKING control of the recorder from its central and marked position.

Try re-adjusting TRACKING and see if this solves the problem. If it does not, and the 'snow' persists beyond the transition between two shots, then the fault may lie elsewhere.

First check the sound-track as well - if it sounds like a lunatic duck, then the chances are you are trying to replay an LP tape on a machine not designed to operate at the lower tape speeds needed for this mode.

If the sound-track sounds relatively normal, then the chances are that the tape transport of your recorder has got dirty! **Do not try to clean the machine by hand.**

The best (and I emphasise the *best*) tape manufacturers produce a 'head cleaning tape'. Try using this, but **follow the instructions carefully.**

If all this fails to clear up snowy pictures, then consult the servicing department of your local retailer.

The sound-track is swamped with rumbling noises.

Most usually, this is caused by wind, or by of puffs of breath hitting the microphone.

The rumbling may be partially cured by putting a 'wind sock' over the microphone. This is a sponge plastic cover that breaks up the impact of the wind on the body of the microphone and reduces the noise.

Unfortunately, it may not be completely effective, so care may be needed to shield the microphone from the direct blast of the wind.

The noise will be more noticeable with omni-directional types of microphone, than with directional types, so experiment by swopping them around.

Occasional puffs of breath hitting a microphone when it is being used for recording a speech, will produce a pronounced 'thump'. The sponge cover will help to reduce the problem, but it is better to get the speaker to move away from the microphone, and to speak across it, rather than directly into it.

Should I have used Hi-Fi sound?

Some VCRs offer what is called Hi-Fi sound. This is an addition to the normal linear sound-track available on a VHS, 8mm or Beta tape. It is of very much higher quality - something which is very noticeable if the replay machine is linked to a hi-fi system.

However, few camcorders will record a hi-fi sound-track, through there are a number of portable VCRs that offer this feature.

Hi-Fi table model VCRs always offer stereo, whereas the ordinary sound-track is normally mono and only sometimes stereo.

Apart from the obvious quality differences that a hi-fi sound-track will bring, the losses that naturally occur when transferring from one tape to another are less noticeable with the hi-fi track, than with the normal sound-track.

Therefore, the answer to the question posed at the beginning is that it may be worthwhile using the hi-fi recording feature for duplicates of your master tape. However, the normal sound-track should be used during the compiling and editing of the final master tape.

10
High-days and Holidays

Special Occasion Video Guide

So far, we have concentrated on a family wedding as the subject of a possible family video record. This event was particularly chosen because it is one of the most complex subjects to record as your first family video film. It provides examples of a wide range of problems and solutions that might be encountered when recording other subjects.

For example, in one production, it faces you with the task of coping with indoor and outdoor scenes, situations where the sound track is only partly scripted and where limited time, no rehearsals and widely separated locations mean the you have plan everything down to the last detail, and yet still be prepared for the unexpected.

All this has reinforced the necessity for careful preparation and the creation and use of a storyboard.

However, once you have caught the 'bug' for using a video camera, you will undoubtedly consider the idea of recording other high spots among the personal experiences of your family and friends. These may be nothing more than a record of a happy gathering, or something larger such as a family event or even a holiday.

In such a case, although you may have gained excellent experience by starting with a wedding video film, new problems may have to be faced where the planning and preparation needed for the wedding video record becomes superfluous – or in many cases just not possible.

Nevertheless, the results of your recordings will not be seen as a credit to you by family viewers and home 'film' critics unless you demonstrate in the rest of your recordings, that you have truly understood the basic elements which make a well-rounded and complete video record.

Exactly what those elements are will be described shortly, but first let us take a look of the kind of alternative video films you might make.

Parties are an obvious choice, not only the sort that are organised for adults, but more importantly, the ones especially for children. These may mark a birthday, some special achievement, or perhaps a home-coming.

In fact, the very growth and development of our children can be the subject of an omnibus serial that will grow from one year to the next. By setting a pattern and style to the first video recording which is duplicated on subsequent occasions, a whole series of short films can be edited together at the end of each year, into a real video album.

However, it is this type of video record which is most likely to come unstuck simply because it deals with very personal events. It is rather like the family slide show that shows little Emily at birth, christening, first birthday party, going to school, and so-on - and totally bores the viewers.

When compiling a video album, bear this in mind and be ruthless in editing out repetitive material. Also, consider the possibility of dubbing a voice-over sound-track that is superimposed on the existing sound recorded by the video camcorder, and adds continuity, humour and interest to the whole production.

Video recordings may also be made of sports, pastimes, historic occasions, nature - indeed, a host of subjects, but they all need to be compiled in a way that will interest an audience outside the bounds of your own family and friends.

One subject which, like the wedding encompasses ideas and techniques which can be 'borrowed' for use in all kinds of other productions, is the annual holiday.

This is because the mood of the 'players' in your recording is invariably light hearted; the holiday location is very different to everyday experience and third, a holiday will often give rise to spontaneous experiences well outside every-day life and which are worth keeping a record of.

Planning on the move

This is where we begin to run into problems. A holiday is nothing like a wedding. The events, apart from the travelling arrangements and destination, are rarely planned. For that matter, none of the players have any kind of scripting as is the case when recording a church ceremony, and finally, often everyone is in a location which, for

Special Occasion Video Guide

practical reasons, cannot be visited in advance.

Trying to make a coherent plan from this is almost impossible. Thus, the storyboard technique, which must normally be based on previous research, visits and experience, is just not practical.

How then can you ensure that you have everything needed to make a complete story-telling record that will keep the viewers happy and amused?

This can only come from a firm understanding of the very necessary and basic elements that ensure completeness and give some theme to the finished production.

Simply stated, any *complete* home video record must have a clear beginning which introduces the viewer to the players and establishes the theme and reason for the recording.

This is followed by the central core which can have a much less organised structure and will often consist of a series of unrelated highlights from the holiday. However, it must be rounded off with a clearly defined end section.

This may seem a statement of the obvious, but in fact many amateur video recordists still make the fundamental mistake of leaving the beginning or the end off their production!

Let me explain. You take a summer holiday, overseas and by the sea. Naturally as an enthusiastic video cameraperson, you take the video camera - but the first time you use it is when you get on the sunny beach at your destination!

This is not a beginning, but really part of the core of the holiday record. To give the video film a proper beginning, you should have started by showing something of the preparations for the holiday, or the journey to the destination.

Planning beyond the necessity for recording all three parts of the video film is, of course, completely impossible - even if you are familiar with the location. However, you still need to keep in mind that the final and edited version of your production will need to be given a sense of continuity.

Remember, although you and those who enjoyed the holiday

with you may be aware that the record misses out some parts of your total experience, this probably happened because the video equipment was not handy. Ideally, your audience will not be aware of this, simply because you have provided a beginning, a middle linked together by continuity devices, and an obvious conclusion to the recording.

Real cases

The actual starting point of a holiday film may be as early as the initial discussions where the destination was selected. In reality, recording this may not be very practical because of the spontaneity with which such things happen. The next, and perhaps more obvious point to begin the video film is the day when you all set off from home.

Whether it be the loading of a car and the journey by road to your destination, or the taxi ride to the airport followed by airport scenes - or even boarding a luxury cruise liner, these will all obviously be a *beginning* without the need to emphasise the fact on the sound track or in titles.

Sometimes, you may have overlooked the opportunity to use these occasions to mark the starting point for the video recording. In this case, the final point which might represent a reasonably satisfactory start for the video film, is the occasion of your arrival at your destination.

A holiday example

Christmas spent away with several friends in a remote cottage is bound to be an occasion which will leave you all with amusing and happy memories - often made even more colourful through the snapshots taken at the time.

How much better if the family photo album is augmented by a video recording of some of the highlights.

This in fact, was the subject of a video film I made recently, so perhaps the reader will excuse me for using this as another example to illustrate the pitfalls and problems that may arise and which are not normally part of the more formal occasion encountered when recording a wedding.

It is worth bearing in mind that although a Christmas holiday is being described, it could equally be a holiday anywhere

Special Occasion Video Guide

at any time of the year. The ideas given here, are merely illustrations of how logical story-telling can be the 'glue' which will make a worthwhile family video film.

The holiday started with a car journey from London to a tiny hamlet in Devon. From the very beginning there moments that were so obviously filmatic that the camera was used from the start.

The car used had very limited space, but because the holiday was being taken during a period when shops were not open, more luggage than usual had to be squeezed into an impossibly small volume.

One of the worst problems was ramming the turkey into place, on top of Christmas parcels, decorations, bottles of Christmas drinks and lots of warm clothes! It was a perfect occasion to record material which would act as the start for the finished production.

Nevertheless, there were practical problems, not the least of which was the chance that something might be missed! Additionally, editing the recording to make something crisper, shorter and with more point, meant that the camera had to be moved from long-shot to close-up, and to a variety of of angles.

For several reasons which will become clear, the camera was run continuously for about ten minutes, and changes of angle, or movement closer or away from the action was achieved using a dollying technique.

Obviously, mounting the camera on a moveable platform in such a situation is hardly practical. However, it is possible to walk slowly with the camera, taking care to avoid any sudden movements that may cause the viewer's eyes to destabilise.

Anyone who has tried to do this will know, that even when walking slowly, there are some body movements transmitted to the camera which seem unavoidable. It is quite natural for the body to rise and fall as each step is taken - and this is very obvious when seen through the lens of the camera.

How do professional camera operators get over this difficulty? The solution is surprisingly simple - but does need some practice! It is nothing more than to adopt a

High Days and Holidays

Groucho Marx style of walking where the knees are kept permanently bent. In this way the camera retains a stable height above ground, just as if it were attached to a mobile dolly truck.

In the opening sequences of the Christmas video described here, a continuous shot of about five minutes duration, showed close-ups of the packed state of the car and still more things arriving to be loaded inside. To these, were added long shots of the state of the car springs and the continual coming and going of the unfortunates responsible for loading.

When carefully edited, this finally provided about two minutes of material which, when backed with carefully chosen music mixed with the live sound track, have subsequently kept many viewers laughing for quite a long time.

The opening section of such a video film is still not complete until the journey itself has been somehow woven into the record. One way of doing this is to film a 'mock start' in which the car is seen disappearing down the road. Of course, because the camera will be wanted for the rest of the holiday, you will have to return to retrieve it - and probably the operator as well!

An alternative, which takes a little less effort, is to record the departure through the car windows. If this is the chosen technique, you will need to be aware that filming through the windscreen or the rear window will always reduce the problems of relative motion between you and nearby objects.

Typically, the impression of motion is given by observing the way in which things pass by. If you film through a side window, close objects appear to move quite fast - even appearing to be a blur if the car is moving quickly. On the other hand, filming from the front or rear windows usually means that objects outside the car are at a greater distance and so the effects of relative motion are less confusing.

Again, camera motion can be a problem. Reduce this by first ensuring the zoom lens is at the wide-angle setting - this can also solve many problems concerning focus. Both near and far objects will remain relatively well focused if the lens is adjusted to the infinity

153

Special Occasion Video Guide

setting and switched to manual.

Recording while the car is in motion can also be uncomfortable for the camera user if the road surface is rough. In this case, the camera should be held free of the shoulder and head by a few inches to avoid the eye being bumped against the viewfinder, and to add extra shock-absorption for the camera.

If there is little conversation in the car during recording, playing the car radio will add extra life and immediacy to the sound track.

The last few hundred yards of the journey, if recorded, will provide a real continuity shot which will also 'key' the viewer into your own reactions to the locale of the holiday site - in this case, a small cottage in a farm-yard at the end of a very narrow and bumpy Devon lane.

However, two new problems arose in the real example being used here. First, it was dark, and second the road surface was so bad that in places, the bottom of the car was scraping the centre of the track!

Even in the dark, it proved to be a good opportunity for the camera to be switched on. By focusing on the lights of the instrument panel - and hoping they were bright enough to record on the tape, some drama was added from the unpleasant sounds of the car grounding - and the expletives of the passengers!

This is a situation where good pictures were unnecessary - and indeed, if the screen had been blank and the only thing happening was on the soundtrack, it would have been quite enough.

The core of the video film

The important, central part of this video film is the holiday proper. Here, the use of the camera can be more haphazard, except that some effort should be made to ensure that plenty of link-shots are recorded.

Linking together scenes of activity is often best done by interspersing them with 'atmosphere' shots. In this case, this comprised scenes of the farmyard, the surrounding scenery and the cottage itself.

Indeed wherever you visit

during your holiday, shots like this, cut between recordings of you and the family at play, will lend a feeling of 'place' and continuity to the complete production.

In our Christmas film example, some of these shots were of the illuminated Christmas tree, piles of decorative parcels, the bowls of fruit and nuts and the room decorations. Further 'fill' shots included close-ups of cows chewing the cud - very useful to add humour to other shots taken later at the Christmas dinner table!

As with the wedding video, cuts in the sound track as the scene changes from one shot to another merely emphasis the cut. Since it is unlikely that you will have a wild-sound recorder with you to enable sounds to be edited across scene changes at the post-production stage, particular care has to be taken to only stop the video camera at an appropriate lull in conversation. (Assuming the sound being recorded is of a conversation.)

During English winter months, recording indoors will always bring problems of available light. There are two solutions - first ensure you take extra lighting on holiday with you, or alternatively, just accept that many of the scenes recorded with available light will be of poor technical quality. This need not detract from the actual content and value of the complete production.

The end section

All good films need and end - and yours will be no exception. Logically, it might be that you choose to record the unloading of your luggage when back at home.

If this is the case, then some link must be provided to avoid the big jump from the holiday scenes, to your home. Some aspects of the return journey must be included to give the feeling of the passage of time as well as distance.

Finally, some of the devices suggested for the wedding production, can also be applied recordings of other kinds of events, such as holidays. Still pictures can be cut into the production to replace missing scenes, sounds can be added from recordings made elsewhere or by other people, or captions and sub-titles can be added to give extra information or humour.

Glossary

Audio dubbing

Refers to the replacement of an existing sound track by sound taken from another recording, or by live sound via a microphone.

The new sound may be taken from a record, but make sure you do not contravene copyright regulations. Some records are made which can be used without problems of this kind.

An alternative source of sound for dubbing may be a tape recording or the sound-track of another video recording. Normally, audio dubbing buttons on a recorder only allow you to change the linear sound track and not the hi-fi sound track.

Bear in mind that some connection problems may arise when cabling a stereo sound machine to a mono video recorder. Reference has been made to this in the book but briefly, the difficulty can be overcome by the use of special adaptor leads available from video, hi-fi or electronic component shops.

Back-light

If the subject you are filming is between you and the light source, it is 'back-lit This has the effect of making the subject stand out as a dark sillhouette against a light background. This situation can be modified to render a more detailed image of the subject by adjusting the automatic iris of the camera.

In some cameras, the control is marked IRIS, in others it uses the letters BLC (Back-Light Control).

Beta

A video tape format and recording system invented by Sony. Cassettes recorded with Beta equipment cannot be replayed on a VHS or 8mm video machines.

Black-burst

This legend may appear as a label for a socket on more advanced types of domestic video equipment. It refers to a synchronising signal used to determine the beginning of each frame of the video signal.

During recording with a video camera, it is generated by the camera and is then used by a system having more than one picture source, say an arrangement employing a video mixing console and another camera. In such a case, the black burst signal produced by the master camera will synchronise the output of all the other devices.

The black burst signal is used by the recorder to time the synchronising pulses recorded on the edge track of the video tape, used to control the timing of the replay video head drum.

BNC connector

A special connector reserved for use with coaxial cable carrying video picture signals only. It is differentiated from the type of connector used for signals at TV aerial frequencies since it has a locking collar which ensures the connection is not readily broken.

C-format

A variation of the VHS tape format in which the tape is loaded into a smaller cassette shell. The video and sound signals recorded on the tape, are identical with those found on a normal VHS tape. Thus, using a mechanical adaptor to bring the cassette dimensions up to the standard size, C-format tapes can be replayed on a normal VHS machine.

The C-format cassette is limited to 30 minutes (SP) or one hour (LP).

Camcorder

The combination of a camera and video cassette recorder into a single unit. Camcorders are now available for all tape formats. However, there are considerable variations in the facilities offered by different models.

CCD

An abbreviation frequently applied to video camera technology. It stands for Charge Coupled Device, which is the technical name for an integrated circuit 'chip' capable of converting light into electrical signals.

It is considerably smaller and consumes less power than the alternative which is based on radio valve technology and commonly called a 'tube'.

CCD's are at an early stage of evolution and improvements are being made all the time. In some models the resolution is not as good as that of a tube. However, CCD's do have the

Special Occasion Video Guide

merit that they do not suffer from being exposed bright lights in the same way that some tubes do.

Evidence of temporary or permanent tube damage caused by over-exposure, is a white burn mark appearing on the screen after the light is removed. If camera is moved, the visual effect is rather like a comet which slowly disappears.

Chroma noise

An effect seen on the screen of a colour monitor or TV set when the colour part of the video signal is below the threshold for good reproduction. The noise manifests itself as a 'rainstorm' of moving coloured spots covering any area of the picture occupied by a dense colour – usually red or blue.

Cocktail party effect.

A term used by the medical fraternity describing the ability of the human ear and brain to focus and interpret a single sound source from an otherwise noisy background. Typically this is most observable in the ability to listen to a particular

conversation in the middle of the sort of hubbub encountered at a party.

Colour temperature

A scale of temperature, expressed in degrees Kelvin. It describes the coloured spectrum of light produced by a hot body.

Low values are coloured red, higher values are blue, and the highest value results in white light – the spectrum produced by bodies such as the sun.

Comet tails

Unpleasant white or coloured streaks that trail over the television screen, tracing the path taken by a bright light source when the camera or light source has been moved.

The trails are transient and indicate that the sensitive surface of the imaging device in the camera has been exposed to a light level beyond the design limits.

Continuity

The technique that forms part of planning and editing to ensure the concentration and attention of the viewer is not

Glossary

disturbed by sudden breaks, changes or omissions in the content of the production.

The transition between one shot and the next is the most difficult to bridge successfully. It may be achieved either with the use of a continuous sound track running through the visual edit point, or by deliberate visual effects such as a fade, dissolve or a rapid pan.

A variety of other techniques have been described in earlier chapters of this book.

Cross-fade

One scene is faded to a blank screen to be immediately replaced by the next scene which is faded in. This normally has to be planned so that the fades are imposed by the camera at the beginning or end of a shot. It is possible to achieve the same effect with a mixing disk, but normally will only be available as a piece of purchased equipment, rather than being hire.

Colour monitor

This looks like a television set but does not have the necessary tuner sections which enable it to decode pictures directly from a TV aerial. The monitor has to work from a VCR or a camera and is driven either by video signals or by what is called a RGB (Red, Green, Blue) signal.

Cut

An abrupt start or finish to a shot. This is the simplest way of creating an edit point between two scenes and can be implemented either with the camera, or during editing. The term refers to the technique employed by a photographic film editor who will literally cut and splice two pieces of film together to obtain the right effect.

Depth of field

A camera lens can only focus at one chosen distance from the lens. However, there is a region in front and behind this point where the picture image may appear to be acceptably focused and it is this region that is called the depth of field. Normally the depth of field is related to the optical design of the lens, but is always dependent on the distance of the main focus point. The closer this is, the smaller the depth of field.

Special Occasion Video Guide

DIN connector

A connector used primarily for audio signal cables and popular with domestic hi-fi equipment. The abbreviation refers to the German standards body responsible for its specification.

Dissolve

An editing technique used to join two shots. It is not an available facility on cameras or camcorders, but may be offered on a video mixing desk. It is achieved by overlapping a fade-in on a fade-out, giving the appearance that the screen is always occupied by an image. Inevitably, the speed of the dissolve, or the differences in the images recorded in the two shots will have a profound effect on the reactions of the viewer.

Dolly

A camera stand on wheels which can be smoothly moved while the camera is in operation. Used as a verb, it describes the action of moving a working camera from point to point.

Fade

A fade is where a picture may be slowly removed to leave a blank screen, or vice versa. The blank screen may be coloured and the speed of the fade adjusted to promote suitable moods among the viewing audience. In some cases, the soundtrack is not faded with the picture, this occasionally being useful to gain a particular effect.

Frame

The moving picture on the TV screen is written by a tiny spot of electrons illuminating the sensitised rear surface of the front plate of the TV tube. The spot travels in a succession of horizontal lines from the top to the bottom of the screen. Two complete scans are required to compile the complete screen image, as each is interlaced with the other. This process takes 1/25th of a second and comprises a complete single frame in the sequence.

Hi-Fi sound

More expensive models of VHS and Beta video cassette recorders are often equipped with the additional feature of hi-fi quality sound.

Insert

This is related to the INSERT button on a video cassette

recorder and describes the replacement of one shot in a video tape, with another. The function of the insert button is first to adjust the position of the tape and recording heads so that the new sequence is precisely synchronised with the existing recorded material. Second the INSERT button can be used to add new/correctly, synchronised material to the end of existing recordings when the tape has been wound from its correct position.

Macro

A lens system that will produce close-ups of relatively small objects. Most zoom lenses fitted to video cameras have a special position, obtained by releasing a catch on the lens barrel, which permits macro views.

Master

In this book, the master tape refers to the tape being used to record the final edited version of the total video film. Any duplicates will be made from the master, rather than trying to edit several identical versions.

Monitor

A TV tube with limited electronics and not containing the tuner section that permits reception of TV broadcasts. A monitor may be a large colour screen device, rather like a TV set, or a very small colour or **monochrome** unit used as the viewfinder on a video camera. Normally, large screen monitors are fitted with a video input and an RGB (Red, Green, Blue) input suitable for connection to a variety of auxiliary hardware including some computers, certain models of VCR and a variety of technical instruments.

Monochrome

Literally, a single colour. Normally refers to a black and white picture.

Newvicon

The technical name applied to a certain type of video camera tube.

Noise bars

See also insert and black burst. Horizontal bars of white spots or streaks across the **monitor** or TV screen. They can indicate interference, but more normally

Special Occasion Video Guide

are an indication that the replay tape heads in the VCR are not properly synchronised to the image on the tape. Noise bars are quite normal on all except the very latest and most expensive VCRs, appears when the tape is being replayed either faster or slower than the normal speed. Noise bars that appear at the transition between one shot and the next are usually a reliable indication that the recorder has been wrongly used.

Omni-directional microphone

The technical description applied to a microphone that is equally sensitive in all directions. Often the standard type of microphone fitted to a video camcorder or camera system.

The technical description applied to a microphone that is equally sensitive in all directions. Often the standard type of microphone fitted to a video camcorder or camera system.

Original

A term used by the author to indicate the tape recording produced by the camera or wild-sound recording and from which transfers will be made to the edited master tape.

Overlay

Normally this is a technique used for captions and title sequences, where the text or graphics literally appear to be laid on top of a scene shot by a camera. Although the overlay technique can be used by professionals to make up a composite picture from two sources, most domestic video equipment will only produce overlayed text from a character generator forming part of a camera system, or added on as an optional extra. The character generator will be programmed by the user to overlay text on the picture whenever needed.

PCM

Abbreviation for Pulse Code Modulation. This is a method normally used to encode the signal from a microphone and to convert it into digital information which is more resilient against the effects of tape noise and distortions which may be introduced by the recording or playback processes. The only video camera system offering PCM sound is the 8mm format.

Glossary

However, the soundtrack is only mono and of limited quality: well below that of, say, a Compact Disc.

Phono

This is often used to describe a single-pin audio plug and socket connection suitable for a single sound channel. It is often found on domestic audio equipment and occasionally used in video equipment.

Post-production

All the processes applied to a recording after the moment it has been made. It will include editing, audio-dubbing, titling, captioning and so on.

Radio Frequency (RF)

The signals coming in on a TV aerial are at RF or Radio Frequency. Video cassette recorders will often have to simulate the output of a TV broadcast station and convert the video signals and sound channels to RF in order to replay the tape via a television set. The exception to this situation is where the TV set is fitted with a video input.

Saticon

A technical term describing a modern type of image-sensing tube used in a video camera.

Saturated colours

Colour TV pictures are compiled from three basic hues, red, green and blue which, when mixed in various ratios will reproduce any other colour we can see. A saturated colour occurs when the TV screen is reproducing a colour at its maximum density.

SCART connector

A rectangular connector having the possibility for up to twenty pins and provided on some of the latest VCRs and TV sets. It provides a simple way of connecting stereo sound and video signals. Also referred to as a Euroconnector.

Soft focus

This does not mean 'out of focus', but a perfectly focused but diffused image giving a slightly ethereal quality to the picture. It may be produced by a lens accessory, or by holding a sheet of glass or film smeared with Vaseline, directly in front of the lens.

Starburst

The visual effect of a star radiating from bright reflections or light sources in the picture area. It is produced by a special-effects lens attachment available for certain makes of camcorder or camera system.

Stereo

In this book the term is applied to a sound recording system where two properly arranged microphones record two channels of sound on a video tape, for later reproduction through a stereo audio system. When the sound is recorded and replayed with a correctly arranged system, it produces considerable realism. In most video systems, the two microphones are incorporated in a single case and are correctly oriented to produce a stereo sound image.

Synchronising

See also **black burst** and **noise bars**.
A special control track pulse recorded on a designated track at the edge of a video tape marking the beginning of each video frame. This pulse is used to synchronise the rotation of the VCR's replay head, to the travelling position of the tape in the machine.

Telephoto

A lens that magnifies a distant image more than the lens normally fitted to the camera. Technically it has a longer focal length than the standard lens. One end of the adjustment of a zoom lens will be marked 'telephoto'.

VCR

Abbreviation for video cassette recorder.

VHS

A video tape recording system invented by JVC of Japan, an abbreviation for "Video Home System".

Video

The raw picture signal before being processed for transmission to a TV set. Optionally and unfortunately used to describe both a recording and a VCR!

White balance

To ensure correct colour reproduction from a camera it needs to 'recognise' what should be represented as white. All colours are modified by the colour of the light illuminating them. Normally a camera system is adjusted for daylight illumination and will reproduce a white object as white. However, the same object illuminated by an ordinary electric light bulb will take on a pink cast unless the WHITE BALANCE control is operated. All cameras provide automatic readjustment of colour rendition, within certain limitations (e.g. a camera cannot render a white object white when it is illuminated by a deliberately coloured light!).

Wide angle

A camera lens of shorter focal length than that normally fitted. It gives a wider view than a standard lens and is one extreme of the range of adjustments available on a zoom lens. Very wide angle lenses can produce distortions of the image if the subject is too close to the camera. Care has to be taken to avoid this unless it is deliberately used for effect.

Wild-sound recording

As described in the text of this book, it is a sound recording which is not synchronised to the picture and made entirely separate from the video camera system.

Zoom

A term that has now entered common parlance and describes a lens with an adjustable focal length, giving wide angle views at one extreme and telephoto at the other. Many zoom lenses fitted to video cameras offer a 6:1 focal length ratio, i.e. the focal length at the telephoto extreme is six times that at the wide angle limit. A few video cameras and camcorders offer as much as a 10:1 ratio.

Technical Appendix

This appendix provides a technical insight into a number of aspects of the equipment and tapes used for making video films. Since it is not intended general reading, but as a reference for the more advanced camera user, it goes more deeply into the subject than the other sections of the book.

More about tapes

The magnetic tape used by video cassette recorders is the result of a complex manufacturing process which represents the end-product of detailed and expensive research.

All tapes currently by VCRs is made by coating a very thin layer of tiny magnetic particles, held in place by a complex plastic binder. The density of particles in the original 'paint', together with the type of magnetic material used - and the way they are coated onto the tape, all contribute in different ways to the performance that is finally obtained.

Historically, the first material used as the magnetic particles was ferric oxide and surprisingly, several decades after the manufacture of the first video tape, this is still a popular and much used material.

Naturally, nothing is ever perfect or incapable of improvement and through the years, the methods of making the ferric oxide have improved, producing a more uniformly shaped and sized particle.

The singular benefit of this has been that when used in a magnetic tape, the tape has been better able to retain the recording over a wide range of temperatures.

Another factor influencing the recording is the presence of magnetic fields - which might be natural, or may originate from common equipment used around the house. More modern tapes are better able to withstand the effects of these weak fields.

Something that was a particular problem with early tapes was the way in which the recording on the tape would be affected simply by the magnetic field arising from the next layer of tape in the tape spool. Modern tapes have almost entirely eliminated these problems - certainly to the point where for domestic applications it is minor.

Nevertheless - there is a warning here that should be noted; do not place or store tapes at elevated temperatures (near a radiator for example), or close to the source of a magnetic field - on top of the TV set!

However, it is not just the stability of the recording that has been improved by making better magnetic particles. Other factors such as the brightness (luminance) of the video signal, the colour (chrominance), the quality of the sound track, and the total signal recovered from the tape have all been improved by changes in the types of magnetic particles or the way the coating process has been modified.

Now, ferric oxide is not the only magnetic material used for modern video tapes, pure metal particles, modified ferric oxide (where other metallic components have been added to the chemical structure) and chromium dioxide have all appeared in recent years.

However, in just the same way that a suit can be made from wool, silk, polyester or other materials - and each impart a different set of properties to the finished product - the suit is still a suit!

Modern video tapes are made to offer specific advantages to the user interested in special applications. The needs of a commercial duplicator of video films are different to those of the person who is actually making a video film!

Similarly, if you are a hi-fi fanatic and want to get the best stereo sound quality out of your machine (combined of course with the best pictures), then there will be a tape made for this purpose.

Broadly speaking, domestic applications fall into the following groups:

- Recording and re-recording from television broadcasts.
- Making your own video films with a video camera system.
- Making copies of your own productions from original tapes.
- Recording stereo sound

Technical Appendix

with your picture (usually from a simulcast where a radio station is broadcasting high quality sound from an event, while a TV station is broadcasting the picture and a standard mono sound channel).

• Recording the same sort of event, but on a VCR offering hi-fi sound recording.

A really good manufacturer of video tape will be able to offer a product which is specifically tailored to each of these applications and designed for the machine you have bought.

For example, TDK offer four different types of video tape for the VHS user (and a similar range for the Beta system), each designed to meet specific needs. As mentioned earlier, when you are recording with a camera, go for the best tape in the range.

In the case of 8mm and VHS-C, the choice is restricted, TDK having already opted for the most suitable grade, knowing that the cassette will only be used to record from a camcorder.

Picture and sound problems

It is a sad fact that most of the defects seen and heard from a video recording are the result of a fault in the VCR, or damage to the tape caused by poor storage conditions or mishandling. It is *very* rare for a fault to be the result of a manufacturing defect, unless a cheap tape from a dubious source has been used.

If the tape has been damaged, the fault will usually emerge no matter on what machine it is replayed. Some faults are attributable to the VCR, the TV set or the adjustments of either of these products - in this case, the tape may not be damaged.

In any instance where the picture of the sound is defective, the user is strongly recommended to go through a series of simple fault-location processes before proceeding further.

The most obvious faults are usually visual and are listed below.

• **A white line across the screen. Sometimes the line may be broken and continue across the screen in a different place.**

In the latter case, this is called a 'dropout' and may be caused by a a poor tape surface. The

Special Occasion Video Guide

continuous white line is a rather more severe case of a dropout.

The cause may be a poor quality tape, but is much more likely to be caused by a scratch on the surface of the tape. The scratch is usually caused by rubbish which can accumulate on a guide post or the record - playback heads in the VCR.

If the tape is permanently damaged, the same fault will show up when the recording is replayed on another machine.

This type of fault is better avoided by employing good maintenance practices. Keep the tape transport of the VCR in good condition by cleaning it using a cleaning cassette from a reputable tape manufacturer. If the fault emerges on a new and different tape, return the VCR for professional servicing

• **Momentary break-up of the picture when replayed. Usually seen as a temporary band of white 'snow' across the screen.**

There are several reasons for this defect appearing. It may be poor editing techniques, in which case the defect only appears at the edit point.

However, the tape may have been creased, made dirty or marked in some way. This can happen if the cassette has been loaded when the tape inside is slack. This may arise because you have pulled the tape from the cassette or the tape has become slack after the cassette has been left inside the machine and the machine switched off when the controls were in the record or play mode.

The problem can be avoided by checking the cassette and taking up slack in the tape before using it, and never switching off the VCR with the cassette still inside. (The exception to this rule is when making a video film, in which case, the power may be turned off between shots - providing the tape is not left in the machine for long periods.)

• **Unstable and shaking picture, or bands of white 'snow' across the screen.**

If one edge of the tape is damaged or the tape head is dirty, the picture may become unstable.

The problem can be solved by using a cleaning tape regularly. If the same tape exhibits the problem on several machines, assume that the edge damage is permanent.

• **White 'snow' across the whole screen, perhaps combined with washed-out colours.**

One or more video heads in the VCR are dirty.

Use a cleaning tape to resolve the problem. If the tape has not been damaged, the fault will not re-emerge.

Cassette storage

Your valuable recording will remain in good condition for many years if you observe a few simple rules.

• Keep the cassette in its storage case and store vertically like a book.
• Do not keep the tape in a hot or moist place or where it might get wet. Avoid storing them in sunlight - this particularly applies to the dashboard or parcel shelf of a car.
• Avoid strong magnetic fields. Typically, these will be on or close to the case of a hi-fi speaker, electric motor (such as that in a vacuum cleaner) or a permanent magnet such as the type children play with, or might be used as decorations on the door of a refrigerator. These can partially erase the tape.
• Try not to drop a cassette or subject it to vibration. This can lead to problems in the way the tape is transported through the VCR.
• Never leave a tape partially wound - always rewind it after use. Dust and dirt that might get into the cassette will affect the surface, or the tape may become slack if you forget this little rule.
• Acclimatise a tape in the place you intend using it. Sudden changes of temperature or humidity (or both) may cause condensation on the tape which will lead to it sticking on the video head drum and cause tape damage, leave garbage in the machine and subsequently affect other tapes.

In some cases, acclimatisation may take up to two hours.
• Check the way the tape winds itself inside the cassette by looking through the plastic windows provided for this purpose. If the reel is not perfectly smooth, rewind the cassette forwards and back a couple of times.
• Do not leave cassettes on a carpeted floor unless inside

Special Occasion Video Guide

a case. Carpet dust and particles will get inside the cassette, or static charges transferred from the nylon carpeting. Static will attract dust and can affect the way the tape winds.

If the fault persists and is common to many of the tapes you have, arrange for the machine to be serviced.

Inside the camera system

Most of the essential features of a video camera system have been described in earlier chapters of this book. However, it is worth pointing out a few things to be considered when purchasing a new camera system.

First, almost all cameras and camcorders now offer both automatic and manual focusing. However, it is worth remembering that the auto-focusing system may be of a type which does not work in low level light conditions, or where the surface being pictured has no defined lines or shape.

The three principal systems in use are ultrasound, infra-red and contrast comparison.

Ultrasound systems can 'see' in the dark, because sound waves, well above the human hearing range, are generated by the camera which then 'listens' for the echo from objects directly in front of the lens and in the centre of the field of view.

The time difference between sending out the sound wave and receiving the echo is used to calculate the range of the object. The result of this calculation is then used to adjust the lens focus.

Infra-red focusing can also 'see' in the dark and uses a very similar method of measuring the distance to the object in the field of view.

Some cameras check the contrast between light and dark images at the centre of the field of view, by actually analysing the picture on the tube or CCD. This type of focusing system will not work in marginal light conditions, or if the object has a smooth surface, or if the surface lacks contrasts of light and dark.

The lens is adjusted until the contrast of the image is at its maximum (i.e. focused).

Cameras fitted with standard

Technical Appendix

lenses (as opposed to the variety which can accept lenses from 35mm cameras or are supplied with the option of fitting telephoto or extended focal length zoom lenses) have a considerable depth of field at all settings except when switched to MACRO.

This means it is often preferable to manually focus the picture as it can avoid irritating changes of focus caused as the range finding system sees changes in the distance of the object in the centre of the picture.

Manual focusing also avoids the problem of irritating changes of focus caused by the range finding system getting confused, or because the camera is being moved while recording.

Tuning the system

Many television sets and VCRS offer electronic tuning and this should cause little trouble. Similarly, most camcorders and portables are pre-tuned to produce an output on a single TV channel.

However, there are possibilities that the TV set may need manually tuning to this signal. In this case, replay a commercial video cassette and adjust the tuning on the TV set to produce the best picture and sound.

Tuning defects show up as a washed-out and 'snowy' picture, buzzing on the sound channel, or patterning on the picture. Check the TV first.

Some VCRs and camcorders allow the predetermined output channel to be retuned. However, this should be done by a service engineer as it can produce some unexpected difficulties.

Connections made from or to video signal sockets do not require or allow user-tuning.

Tuning is a term that can also be applied to the TRACKING control on the camcorder or VCR. This control should never be moved from its preferred position, usually marked by a detent that can be felt as the knob is moved - unless picture 'jittering' occurs when playing back a tape already carrying a recording.

It should never be moved from the preferred setting during recording (although often it has been disabled in such circumstances).

Index

A
Acclimatising equipment, 84, 171
AGC, 48
Assembly editing, 99
Audio dubbing, 21, 48, 51, 156
Audio, see also Sound
Auto-focusing, 24-5, 44-5, 172-3

B
Back-light, 44, 89, 156
Back-space edit, 123
Batteries, 33-4, 133-4
Beta, 21-2, 156
Black burst, 104, 156-7
BNC connector, 101, 157
Brightness, 27

C
C-format, 21-2, 157
  equipment, 40-7
Camcorders, 20, 35-7, 40-9, 157
Camera motion, 152-4
Camera-recorder combinations, 49-52
Camera-recorder connection, 35-7
Candid camera, 61-62
Caption cards, 106-8, 119-20
  see also Titling
Cars, filming from, 80, 153-4
Cassettes, see Tapes
CCD, 26, 157-8
Ceremony, wedding, 91-3, 139-40
Chroma noise, 29, 158
Cocktail party effect, 32, 158
Colour monitor, 159
Colour temperature, 29-30, 45, 158
Comet tails, 158
Continuity, 17, 72, 74, 158-9
  see also Editing
Contrast, 27
Controls, camera, 40-9
Cross-fade, 159
Cut, 76-7, 159

D
Diagrams, preliminary, 16-18, 62
DIN connector, 160
Dissolve, 160
Dolly, 78-9, 160
Dubbing, 21, 48, 51, 156

E
Editing, 99-127, 140-2
  advanced equipment, 103-6
  combination of aural and visual effect, 121
  minimum VCR specification, 100
  notes, 112-8
  problems, 140-2
  sound, 123
  titling camera, 104
End sections, 58, 96, 106-7, 155
Equipment checking, 84-5, 133-5

F
Fading, 44, 77-8, 160
Fill-ins, 68, 70, 87-91, 94, 154-5
Fluorescent lighting, 30
Focusing, 24-5, 44-5, 80-1, 172-3
Full Auto, 43-4

G
Generator lock, 104-6

H
Hi-fi sound, 146, 160
Hosepiping, 79-80

I

Incidental shots, see *Fill-ins*
Indexing of shots, 112
Insert editing, 99, 142, 160-1
Iris system, 27-8, 48

J

Joins, 141

L

Labelling, 84
Lenses, 24-6
Lettering, 102-3
Lighting, 53-5, 62-4, 135-7
LP, 42, 43
Lux, 26

M

Macro, 24, 42, 161
Master tape, 113, 161
Memory, 43, 143.
Microphones, 41-3, 46, 47, 65, 95, 134-5, 145-6
Mistakes, 70-1, 130-46
Monitors, 34-5, 42, 46, 161
Monochrome, 161

N

Newvicon tubes, 26, 161
Noise bars, 123-4, 161-2
Notes, 13, 16-18, 69-70, 92, 93, 95, 131-2
    editing, 112-8

O

Omni-directional microphones, 31, 162
Original tape, 113, 162
Overlay, 118, 162

P

Panning, 28, 75-6
PCM, 65, 162-3
Phono, 163
Picture
    insert, 51
    quality loss, 144-5, 169-71
Power supply, 33-4
Preparation
    on the day, 84-7
    on the move, 149-51

R

Radio frequency (RF), 37, 163
Rec review, 45
Reception, wedding, 93-7
Record-Pause, 42, 142
Recorder camera connection, 35-7
Reset counter, in editing, 143-4

S

Saticon tubes, 26, 163
Saturated colours, 29, 163
SCART connector, 101-2, 163
Sensing the image, 26-9
Simulcast, 53
Sketches, 16-8, 62
'Snow' 170-1
Soft focus, 26, 163
Sound, 64-8
    combination of aural and visual effect, 121
    editing, 122, 124-7, 145-6
    problems, 169
    systems, 21, 31-3, 47-8
    see also *Microphones; Wild sound recording*
SP mode, 43
Starburst, 26, 164
Stereo, 33, 47, 164
Stereo-to-mono connectors, 112-3
Storyboard, 13, 16-18, 69-70, 92, 93, 95, 131-2
Synchronising, 104, 123-4, 164

Index

T
Tape counter, in editing, 143-4
Tapes
   selection, 38, 52-3
   storage, 171-2
   technical aspects, 167-9
Telephoto, 24, 164
Television, 49-52, 99-110, 144, 173
Testing equipment, 84-5, 133-5
Titling, 58, 106-10, 118-22
Titling camera, 104
Tricks, 71
   see also *Editing; Mistakes*
Tripods, 49, 137-8
Tuning, 173

V
VHS, 22, 164
   see also *C-format*

W
White balance, 30, 48, 164-5
Wide angle, 24, 165
Wild sound recording, 15, 66-7, 74, 165
Wild vs *synchornised sound,* 124-7

Z
Zoom, 24, 42, 79-80, 165